5 | EL CAKR

STORY : CORBEYRAN
ART : DJILLALI DEFALI
COLOR : CYRIL VINCENT

Also available
1. DESMOND
2. AQUILUS
3. ACCIPITER
4. HAWK

ASSASSIN'S CREED: EL CAKR
ISBN: 9781783293582

Published by Titan Books
A division of Titan Publishing Group Ltd.
144 Southwark Street, London SE1 0UP

First Titan edition: November 2014
English-language translation: Mark McKenzie-Ray

A CIP catalogue record for this title is available from the British Library

10 9 8 7 6 5 4 3 2 1

Printed in China

Thank you to Amy, François and Matz.
CORBEYRAN

A huge thank you to François for your years of collaboration.
You are not just a colleague, but a true friend. Thank you,
buddy, and good luck for whatever happens next.
DEFALI

What did you think of this book? We love to hear from our readers. Please email us
at: readerfeedback@titanemail.com, or write to us at the above address. To receive
advance information, news, competitions, and exclusive offers online, please sign up
for the Titan newsletter on our website: www.titanbooks.com

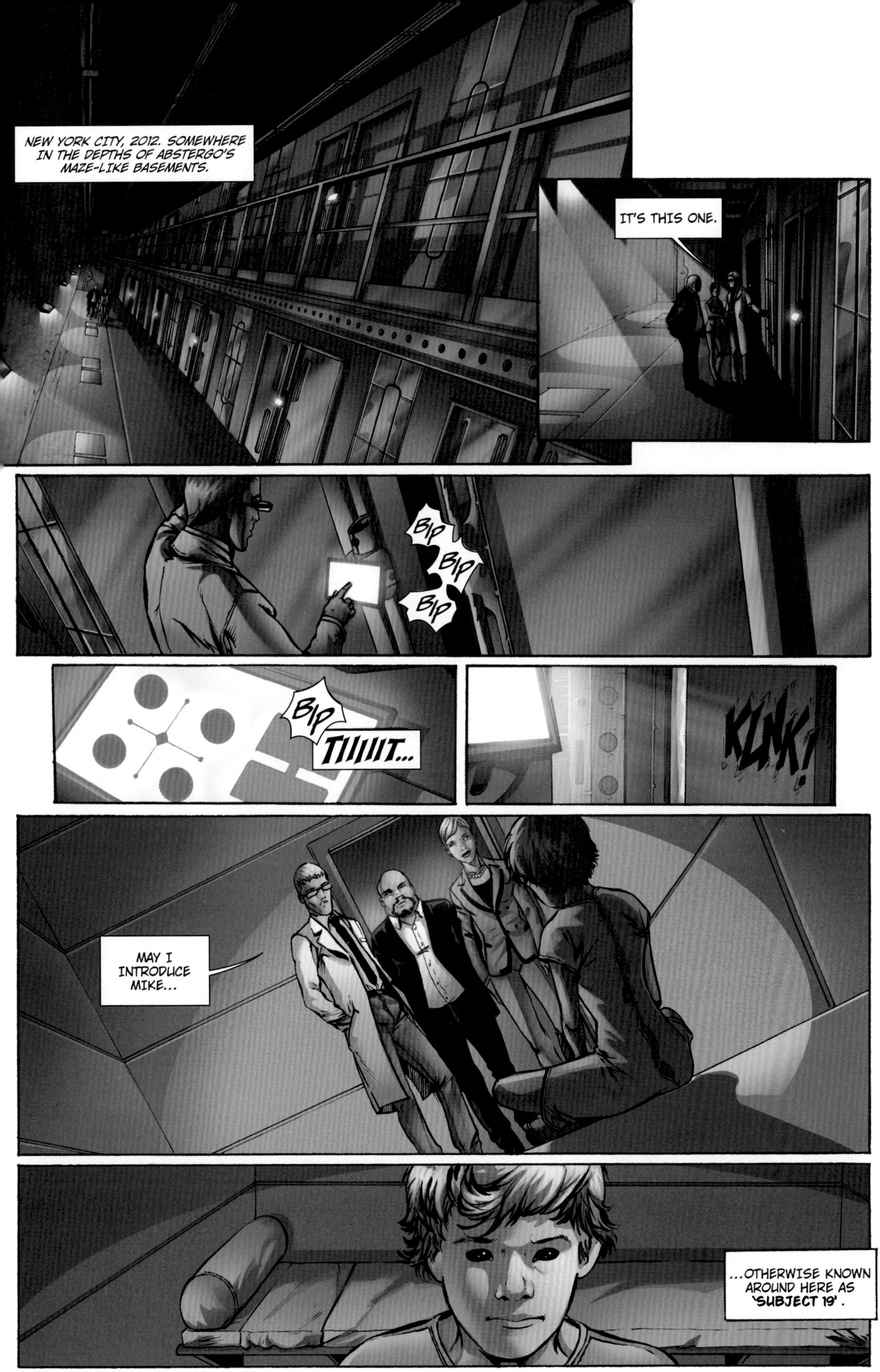
NEW YORK CITY, 2012. SOMEWHERE IN THE DEPTHS OF ABSTERGO'S MAZE-LIKE BASEMENTS.
IT'S THIS ONE.
BIP
BIP
BIP
BIP
TIIIIIT...
KLNK!
MAY I INTRODUCE MIKE...
...OTHERWISE KNOWN AROUND HERE AS 'SUBJECT 19'.

1

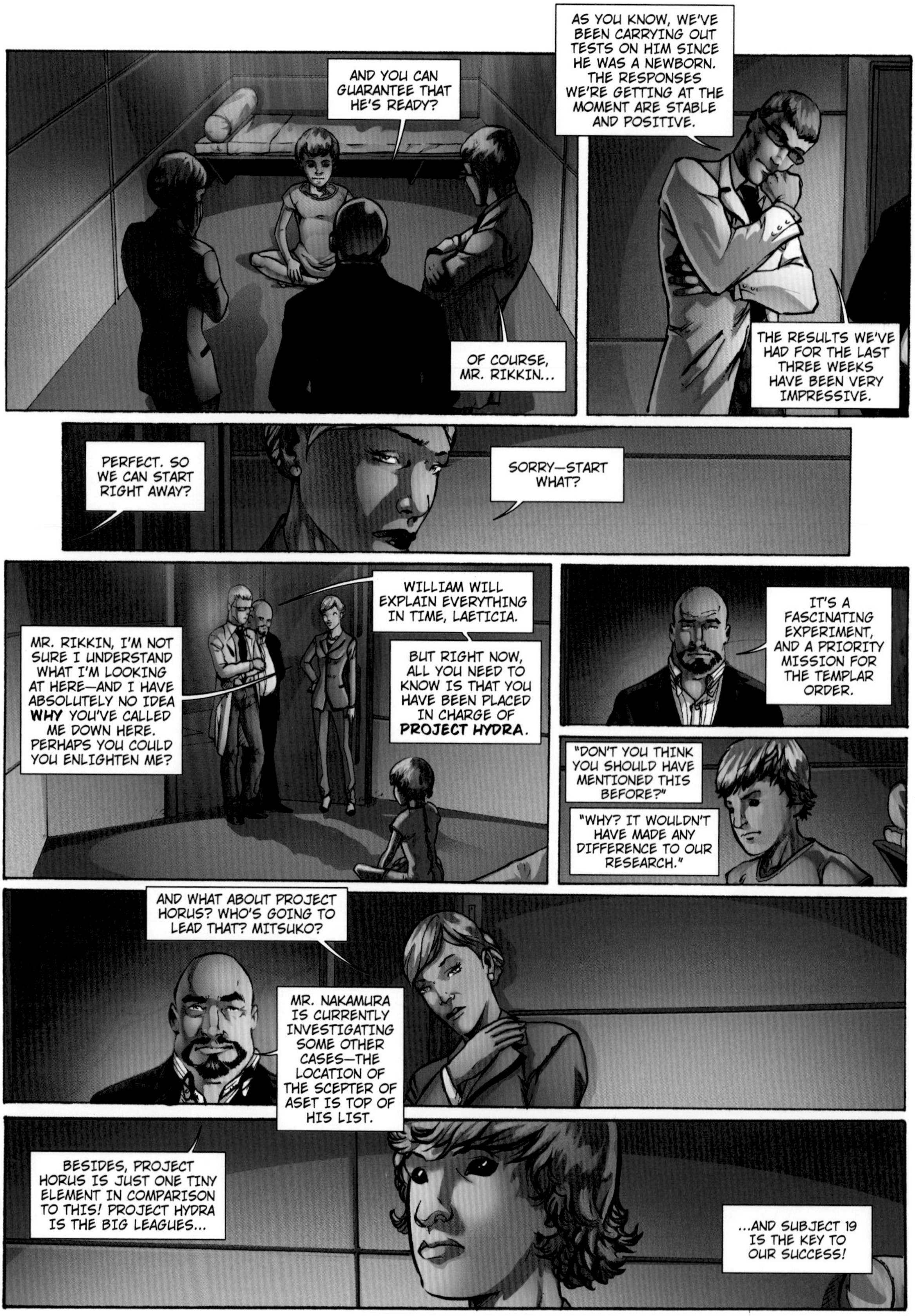
AND YOU CAN GUARANTEE THAT HE'S READY?
OF COURSE, MR. RIKKIN...
AS YOU KNOW, WE'VE BEEN CARRYING OUT TESTS ON HIM SINCE HE WAS A NEWBORN. THE RESPONSES WE'RE GETTING AT THE MOMENT ARE STABLE AND POSITIVE.
THE RESULTS WE'VE HAD FOR THE LAST THREE WEEKS HAVE BEEN VERY IMPRESSIVE.
PERFECT. SO WE CAN START RIGHT AWAY?
SORRY—START WHAT?
MR. RIKKIN, I'M NOT SURE I UNDERSTAND WHAT I'M LOOKING AT HERE—AND I HAVE ABSOLUTELY NO IDEA **WHY** YOU'VE CALLED ME DOWN HERE. PERHAPS YOU COULD YOU ENLIGHTEN ME?
WILLIAM WILL EXPLAIN EVERYTHING IN TIME, LAETICIA.
BUT RIGHT NOW, ALL YOU NEED TO KNOW IS THAT YOU HAVE BEEN PLACED IN CHARGE OF **PROJECT HYDRA**.
IT'S A FASCINATING EXPERIMENT, AND A PRIORITY MISSION FOR THE TEMPLAR ORDER.
"DON'T YOU THINK YOU SHOULD HAVE MENTIONED THIS BEFORE?"
"WHY? IT WOULDN'T HAVE MADE ANY DIFFERENCE TO OUR RESEARCH."
AND WHAT ABOUT PROJECT HORUS? WHO'S GOING TO LEAD THAT? MITSUKO?
MR. NAKAMURA IS CURRENTLY INVESTIGATING SOME OTHER CASES—THE LOCATION OF THE SCEPTER OF ASET IS TOP OF HIS LIST.
BESIDES, PROJECT HORUS IS JUST ONE TINY ELEMENT IN COMPARISON TO THIS! PROJECT HYDRA IS THE BIG LEAGUES...
...AND SUBJECT 19 IS THE KEY TO OUR SUCCESS!

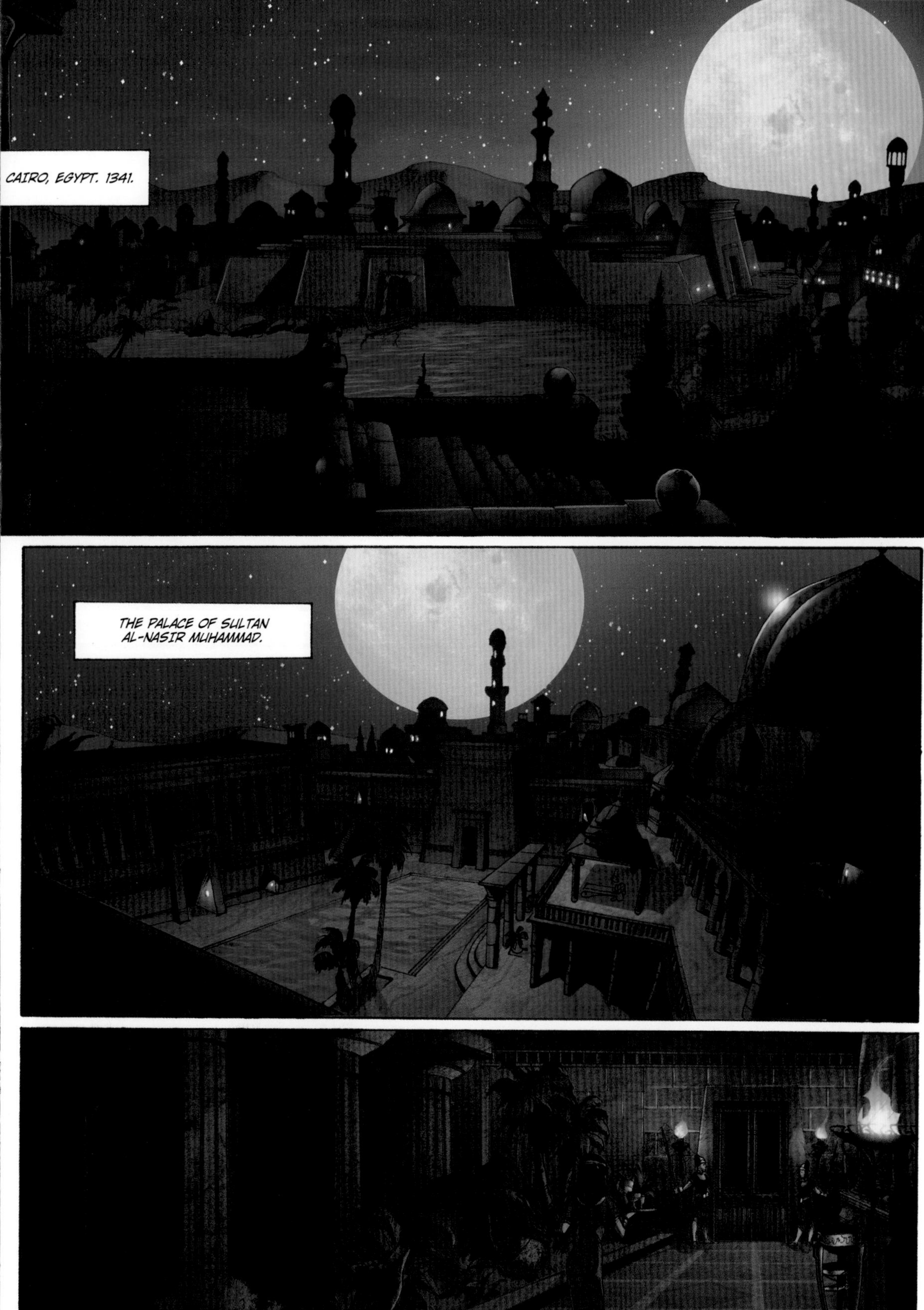
CAIRO, EGYPT. 1341.
THE PALACE OF SULTAN AL-NASIR MUHAMMAD.

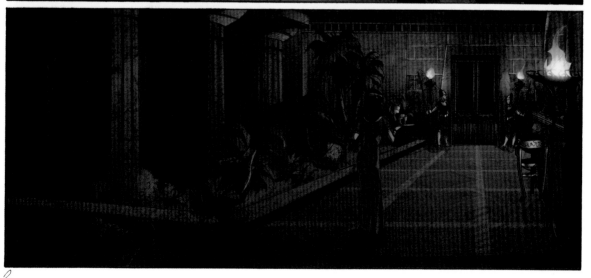

I BRING TEA FOR THE SULTAN.

GOOD EVENING, YOUR HIGHNESS.

LEILA! THE JOY OF MY NIGHTS!

YOUR TEA, MY LORD.

STOP THAT AT ONCE, LEILA! THAT WRETCHED NOISE MAKES ME WANT TO PISS!

COME HERE AND SIT WITH ME INSTEAD. FORGET ABOUT THE TEA.

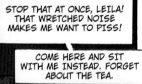

AS YOU COMMAND, MY LORD. I AM HERE TO SERVE YOU.

4

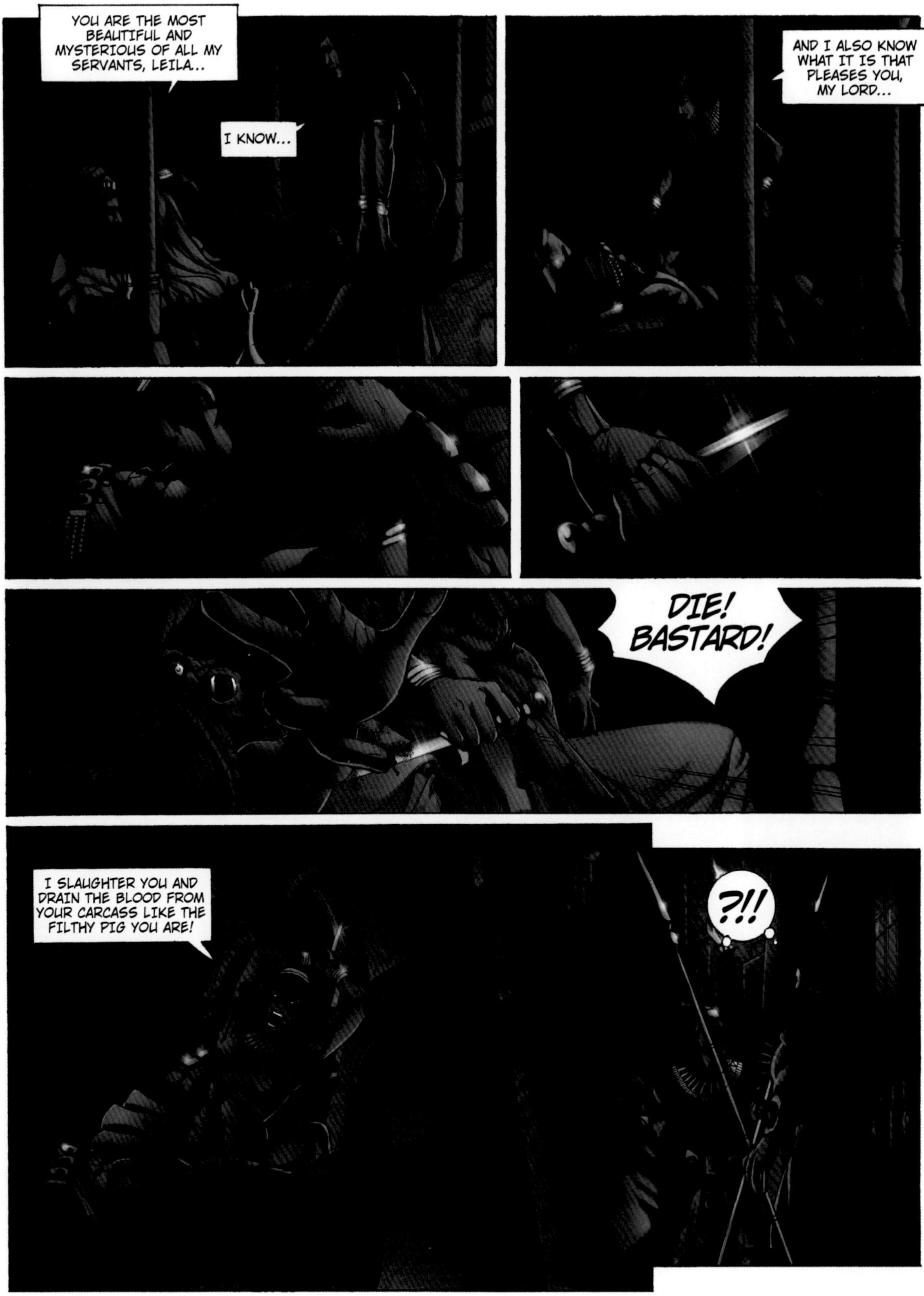
YOU ARE THE MOST BEAUTIFUL AND MYSTERIOUS OF ALL MY SERVANTS, LEILA...
I KNOW...
AND I ALSO KNOW WHAT IT IS THAT PLEASES YOU, MY LORD...
DIE! BASTARD!
I SLAUGHTER YOU AND DRAIN THE BLOOD FROM YOUR CARCASS LIKE THE FILTHY PIG YOU ARE!
?!!

5

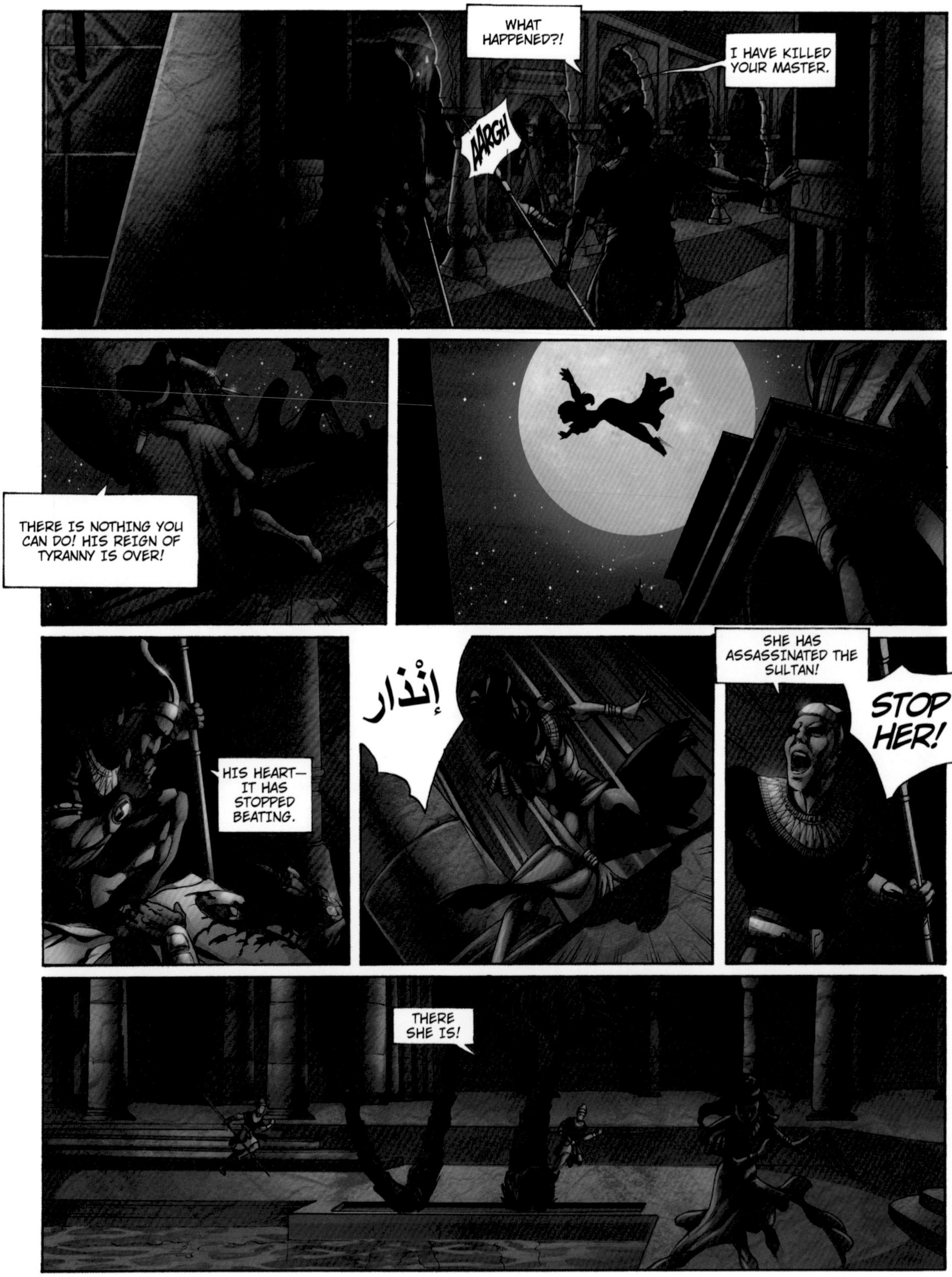
WHAT HAPPENED?!
I HAVE KILLED YOUR MASTER.
AARGH
THERE IS NOTHING YOU CAN DO! HIS REIGN OF TYRANNY IS OVER!
HIS HEART— IT HAS STOPPED BEATING.
إنْذار
SHE HAS ASSASSINATED THE SULTAN!
STOP HER!
THERE SHE IS!

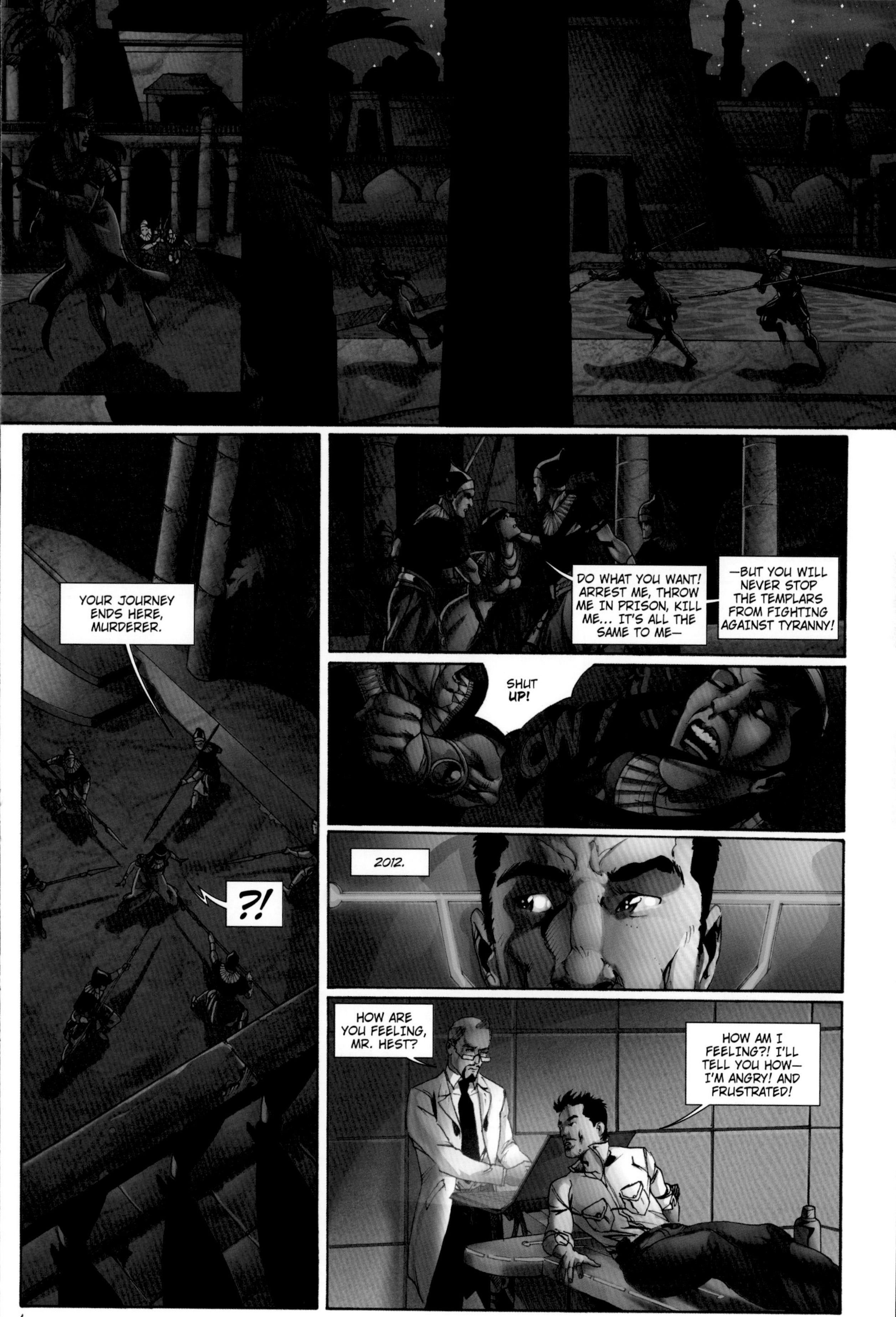
YOUR JOURNEY ENDS HERE, MURDERER.
?!
DO WHAT YOU WANT! ARREST ME, THROW ME IN PRISON, KILL ME... IT'S ALL THE SAME TO ME—
—BUT YOU WILL NEVER STOP THE TEMPLARS FROM FIGHTING AGAINST TYRANNY!
SHUT UP!
2012.
HOW ARE YOU FEELING, MR. HEST?
HOW AM I FEELING?! I'LL TELL YOU HOW— I'M ANGRY! AND FRUSTRATED!

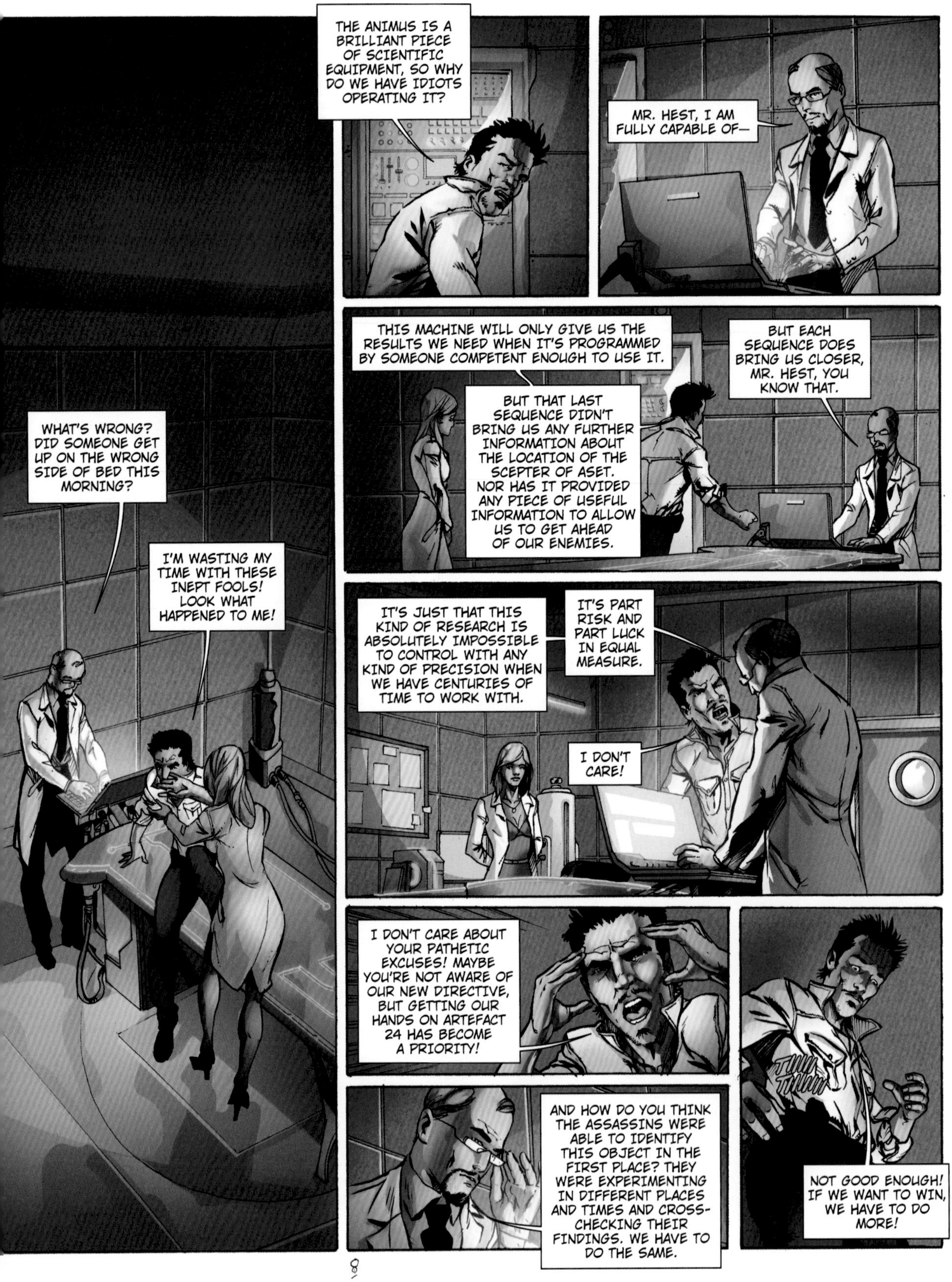

THE ANIMUS IS A BRILLIANT PIECE OF SCIENTIFIC EQUIPMENT, SO WHY DO WE HAVE IDIOTS OPERATING IT?
MR. HEST, I AM FULLY CAPABLE OF—
THIS MACHINE WILL ONLY GIVE US THE RESULTS WE NEED WHEN IT'S PROGRAMMED BY SOMEONE COMPETENT ENOUGH TO USE IT.
BUT EACH SEQUENCE DOES BRING US CLOSER, MR. HEST, YOU KNOW THAT.
BUT THAT LAST SEQUENCE DIDN'T BRING US ANY FURTHER INFORMATION ABOUT THE LOCATION OF THE SCEPTER OF ASET. NOR HAS IT PROVIDED ANY PIECE OF USEFUL INFORMATION TO ALLOW US TO GET AHEAD OF OUR ENEMIES.
IT'S JUST THAT THIS KIND OF RESEARCH IS ABSOLUTELY IMPOSSIBLE TO CONTROL WITH ANY KIND OF PRECISION WHEN WE HAVE CENTURIES OF TIME TO WORK WITH.
IT'S PART RISK AND PART LUCK IN EQUAL MEASURE.
I DON'T CARE!
I DON'T CARE ABOUT YOUR PATHETIC EXCUSES! MAYBE YOU'RE NOT AWARE OF OUR NEW DIRECTIVE, BUT GETTING OUR HANDS ON ARTEFACT 24 HAS BECOME A PRIORITY!
AND HOW DO YOU THINK THE ASSASSINS WERE ABLE TO IDENTIFY THIS OBJECT IN THE FIRST PLACE? THEY WERE EXPERIMENTING IN DIFFERENT PLACES AND TIMES AND CROSS-CHECKING THEIR FINDINGS. WE HAVE TO DO THE SAME.
NOT GOOD ENOUGH! IF WE WANT TO WIN, WE HAVE TO DO MORE!
WHAT'S WRONG? DID SOMEONE GET UP ON THE WRONG SIDE OF BED THIS MORNING?
I'M WASTING MY TIME WITH THESE INEPT FOOLS! LOOK WHAT HAPPENED TO ME!

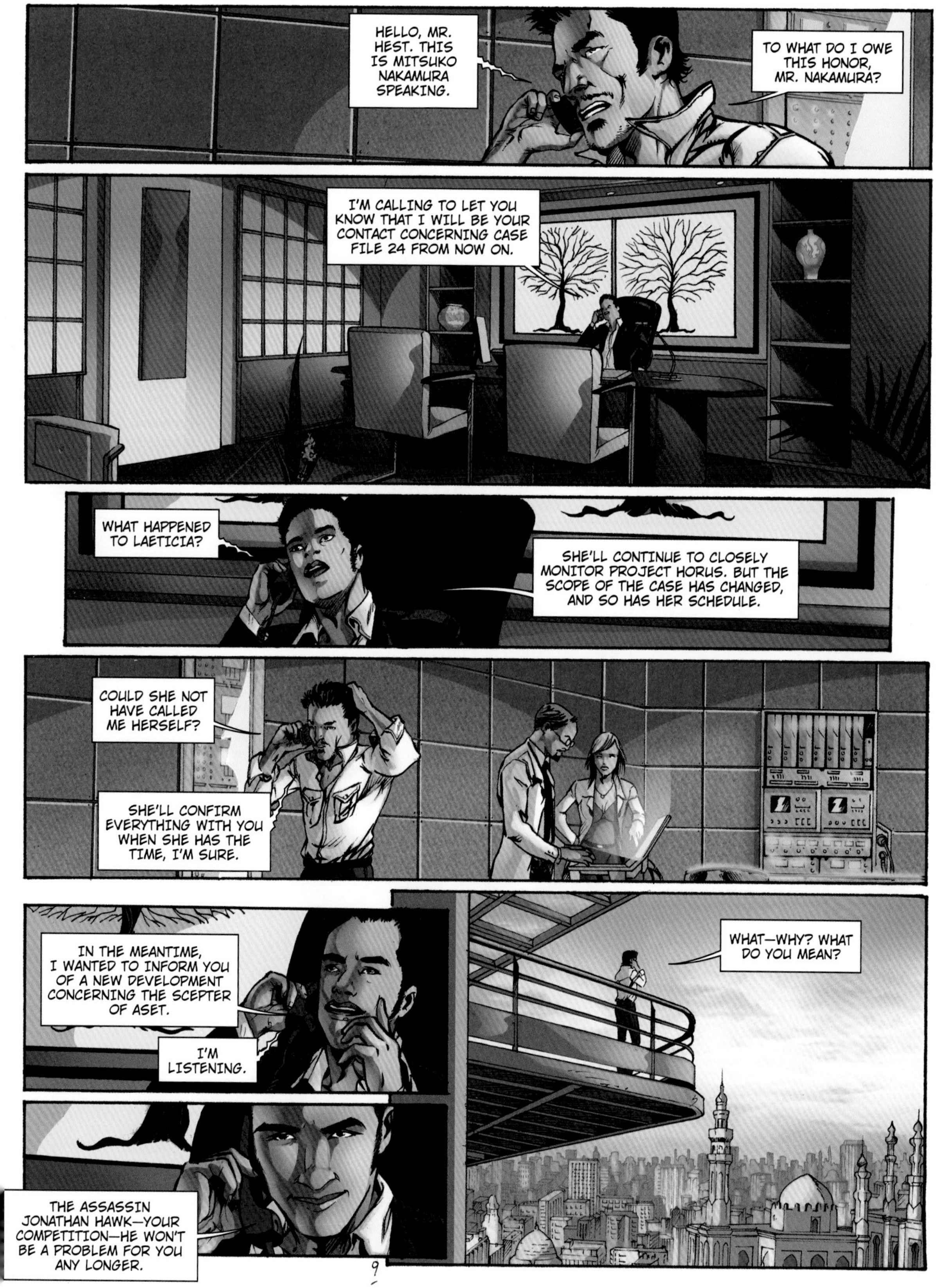
HELLO, MR. HEST. THIS IS MITSUKO NAKAMURA SPEAKING.
TO WHAT DO I OWE THIS HONOR, MR. NAKAMURA?
I'M CALLING TO LET YOU KNOW THAT I WILL BE YOUR CONTACT CONCERNING CASE FILE 24 FROM NOW ON.
WHAT HAPPENED TO LAETICIA?
SHE'LL CONTINUE TO CLOSELY MONITOR PROJECT HORUS. BUT THE SCOPE OF THE CASE HAS CHANGED, AND SO HAS HER SCHEDULE.
COULD SHE NOT HAVE CALLED ME HERSELF?
SHE'LL CONFIRM EVERYTHING WITH YOU WHEN SHE HAS THE TIME, I'M SURE.
IN THE MEANTIME, I WANTED TO INFORM YOU OF A NEW DEVELOPMENT CONCERNING THE SCEPTER OF ASET.
I'M LISTENING.
WHAT—WHY? WHAT DO YOU MEAN?
THE ASSASSIN JONATHAN HAWK—YOUR COMPETITION—HE WON'T BE A PROBLEM FOR YOU ANY LONGER.

OUR MOLE HAS BEEN ASSIGNED TO ELIMINATE HIM. YOU'LL BE THE ONLY SUBJECT RUNNING AROUND EGYPT FROM NOW ON.

UH-HUH.

YOU DON'T SOUND VERY HAPPY. IS THERE SOMETHING I SHOULD KNOW?

HAWK AND I, WE'VE GOT HISTORY—AN OLD SCORE TO SETTLE. BETWEEN YOU AND ME, I'D HAVE LIKED TO HAVE GOTTEN RID OF HIM MYSELF.

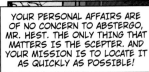

YOUR PERSONAL AFFAIRS ARE OF NO CONCERN TO ABSTERGO, MR. HEST. THE ONLY THING THAT MATTERS IS THE SCEPTER. AND YOUR MISSION IS TO LOCATE IT AS QUICKLY AS POSSIBLE!

I PROMISE YOU THAT I'LL DO MY VERY BEST, MR. NAKAMURA.

AS YOUR NEW HEAD, I WOULD EXPECT NOTHING LESS FROM YOU.

I'LL KEEP IN TOUCH.

THAT'S ALL I NEED.

SHIT.

TIIP

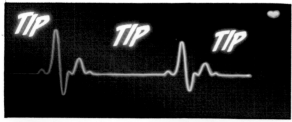

TIP   TIP   TIP

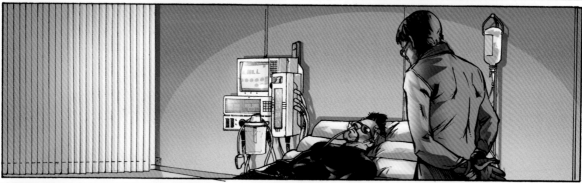

HOW IS HE?

STILL UNCONSCIOUS.

WHAT ARE HIS PROSPECTS? IS THERE ANY HOPE?

FROM A STROKE? WE DON'T KNOW WHAT HIS OUTCOME WILL BE...

...IT'S TOO SOON TO SAY.

WE CAN'T DO ANYTHING MORE FOR HIM. WHAT WE NEED TO DO NOW IS FIND THIS MOLE.

DOES LAETICIA HAVE ANY SUSPECTS?

WELL, SHE DID SAY SOMETHING ABOUT NANCY—

NANCY? WORKING FOR THE **TEMPLARS**? I FIND THAT HARD TO BELIEVE...

11

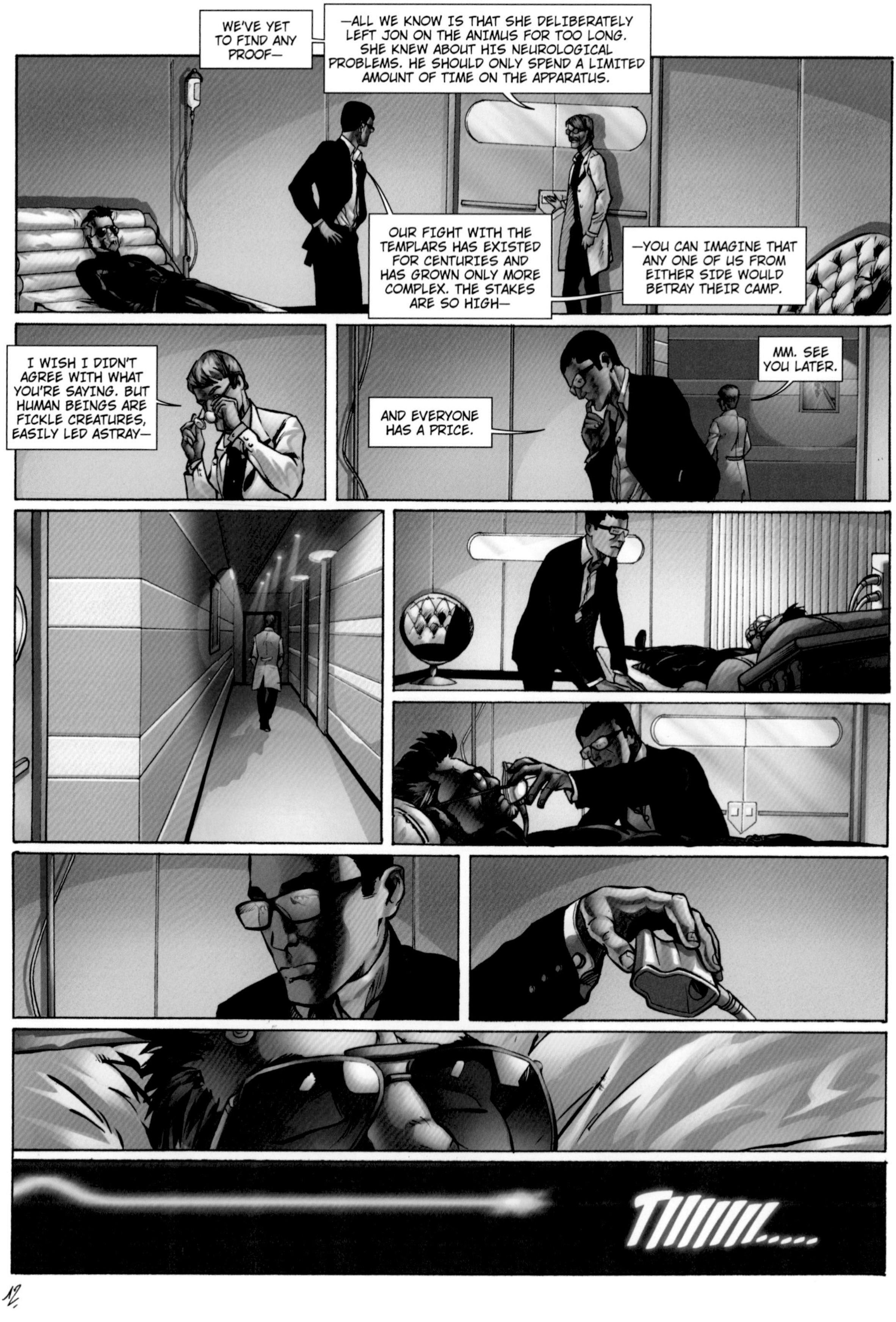

WE'VE YET TO FIND ANY PROOF—
—ALL WE KNOW IS THAT SHE DELIBERATELY LEFT JON ON THE ANIMUS FOR TOO LONG. SHE KNEW ABOUT HIS NEUROLOGICAL PROBLEMS. HE SHOULD ONLY SPEND A LIMITED AMOUNT OF TIME ON THE APPARATUS.
OUR FIGHT WITH THE TEMPLARS HAS EXISTED FOR CENTURIES AND HAS GROWN ONLY MORE COMPLEX. THE STAKES ARE SO HIGH—
—YOU CAN IMAGINE THAT ANY ONE OF US FROM EITHER SIDE WOULD BETRAY THEIR CAMP.
I WISH I DIDN'T AGREE WITH WHAT YOU'RE SAYING. BUT HUMAN BEINGS ARE FICKLE CREATURES, EASILY LED ASTRAY—
AND EVERYONE HAS A PRICE.
MM. SEE YOU LATER.
TIIIIIII.....

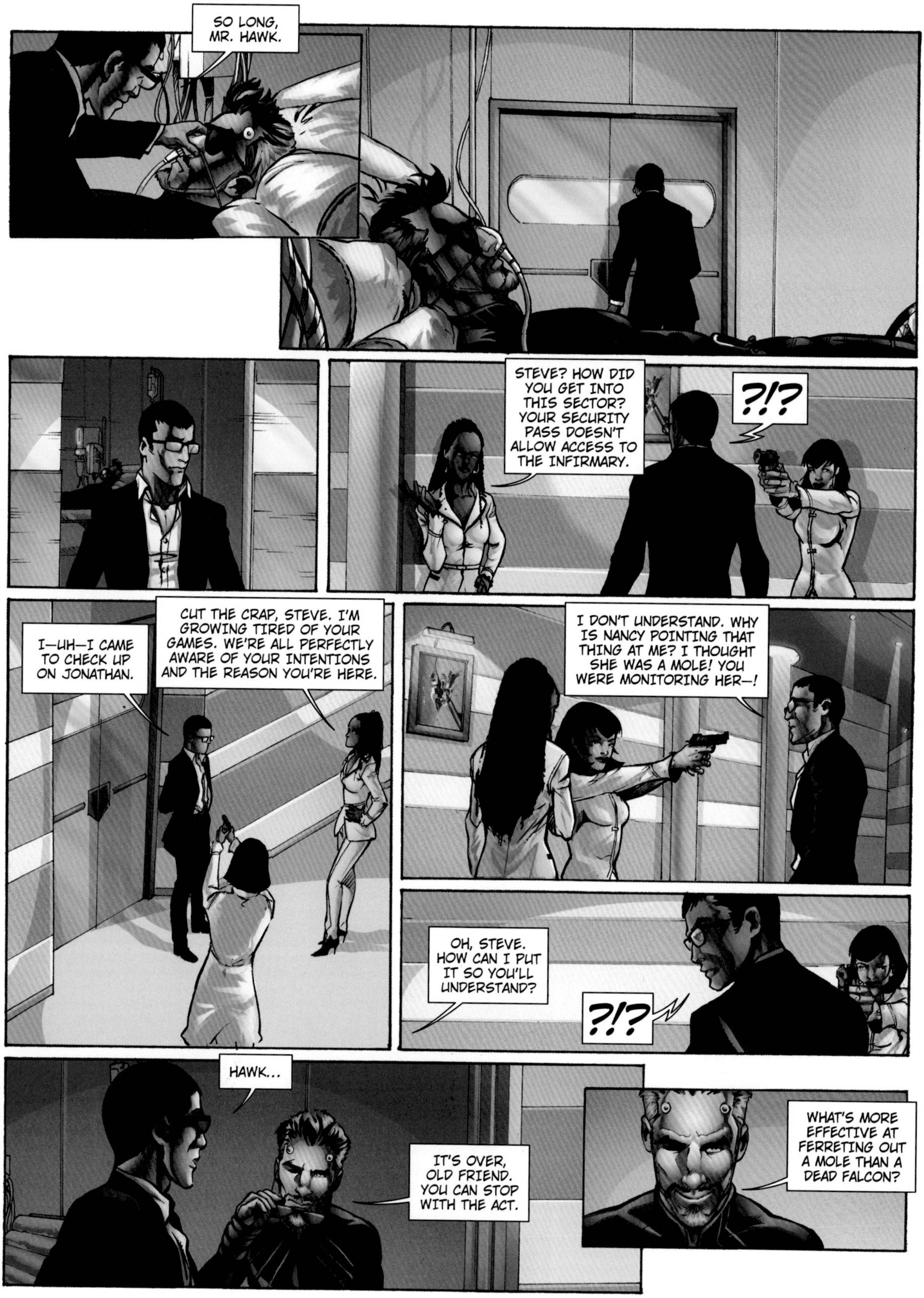
SO LONG, MR. HAWK.
STEVE? HOW DID YOU GET INTO THIS SECTOR? YOUR SECURITY PASS DOESN'T ALLOW ACCESS TO THE INFIRMARY.
?!?
I—UH—I CAME TO CHECK UP ON JONATHAN.
CUT THE CRAP, STEVE. I'M GROWING TIRED OF YOUR GAMES. WE'RE ALL PERFECTLY AWARE OF YOUR INTENTIONS AND THE REASON YOU'RE HERE.
I DON'T UNDERSTAND. WHY IS NANCY POINTING THAT THING AT ME? I THOUGHT SHE WAS A MOLE! YOU WERE MONITORING HER—!
OH, STEVE. HOW CAN I PUT IT SO YOU'LL UNDERSTAND?
?!?
HAWK...
IT'S OVER, OLD FRIEND. YOU CAN STOP WITH THE ACT.
WHAT'S MORE EFFECTIVE AT FERRETING OUT A MOLE THAN A DEAD FALCON?

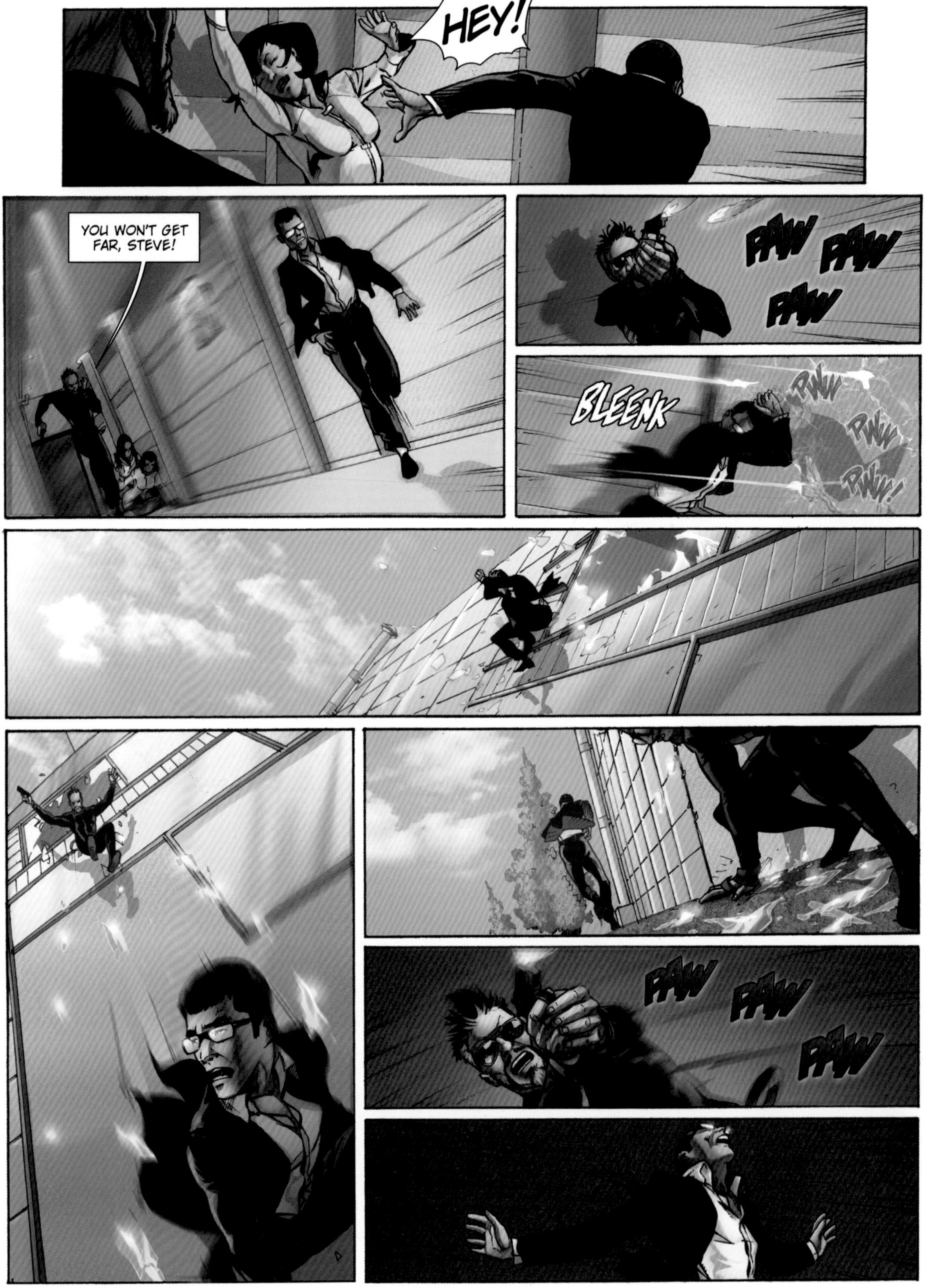
HEY!
YOU WON'T GET FAR, STEVE!
PAW PAW
PAW
BLEENK
PWW
PWW
PWW!
PAW
PAW
PAW

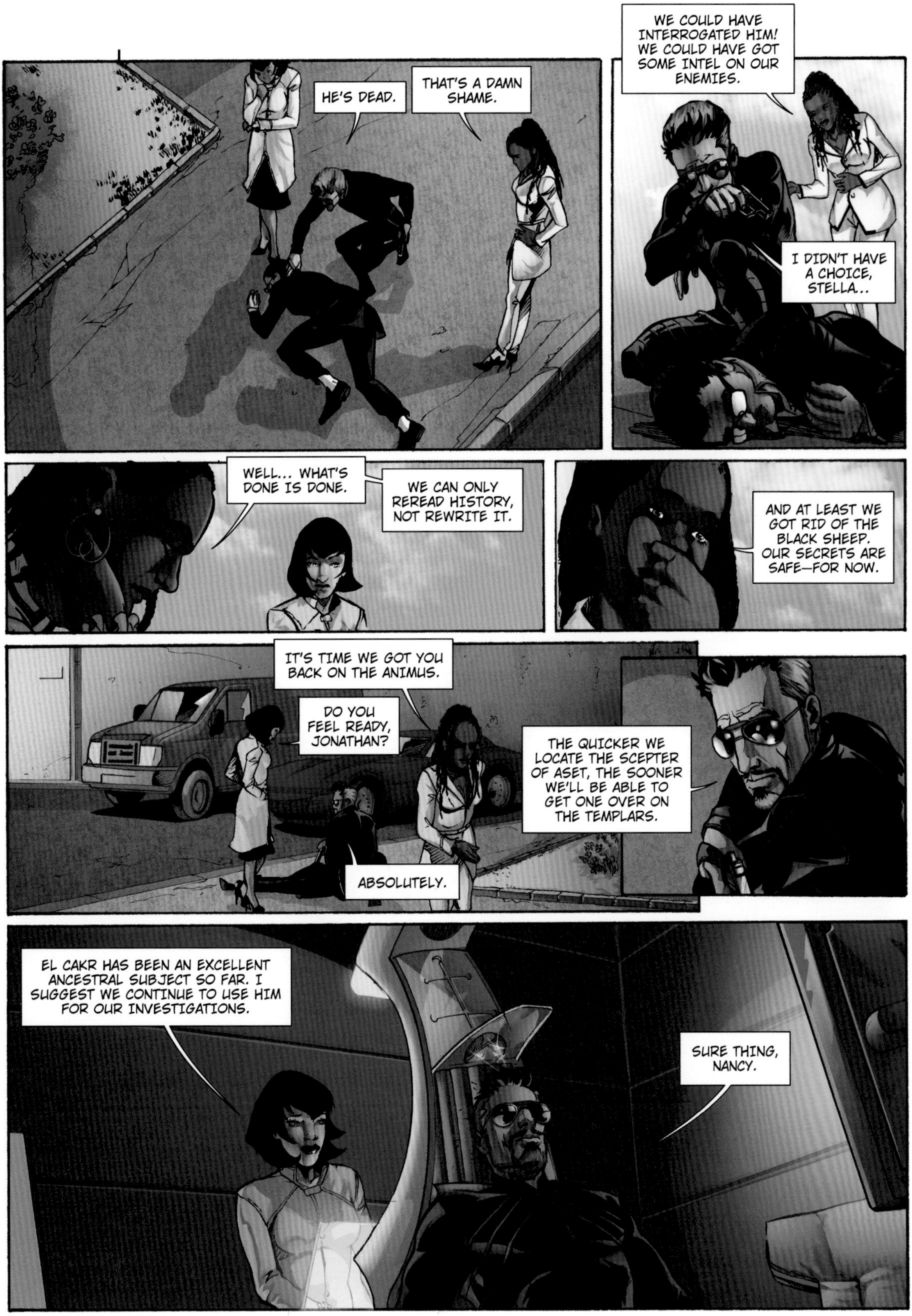
HE'S DEAD.
THAT'S A DAMN SHAME.
WE COULD HAVE INTERROGATED HIM! WE COULD HAVE GOT SOME INTEL ON OUR ENEMIES.
I DIDN'T HAVE A CHOICE, STELLA...
WELL... WHAT'S DONE IS DONE.
WE CAN ONLY REREAD HISTORY, NOT REWRITE IT.
AND AT LEAST WE GOT RID OF THE BLACK SHEEP. OUR SECRETS ARE SAFE—FOR NOW.
IT'S TIME WE GOT YOU BACK ON THE ANIMUS.
DO YOU FEEL READY, JONATHAN?
ABSOLUTELY.
THE QUICKER WE LOCATE THE SCEPTER OF ASET, THE SOONER WE'LL BE ABLE TO GET ONE OVER ON THE TEMPLARS.
EL CAKR HAS BEEN AN EXCELLENT ANCESTRAL SUBJECT SO FAR. I SUGGEST WE CONTINUE TO USE HIM FOR OUR INVESTIGATIONS.
SURE THING, NANCY.

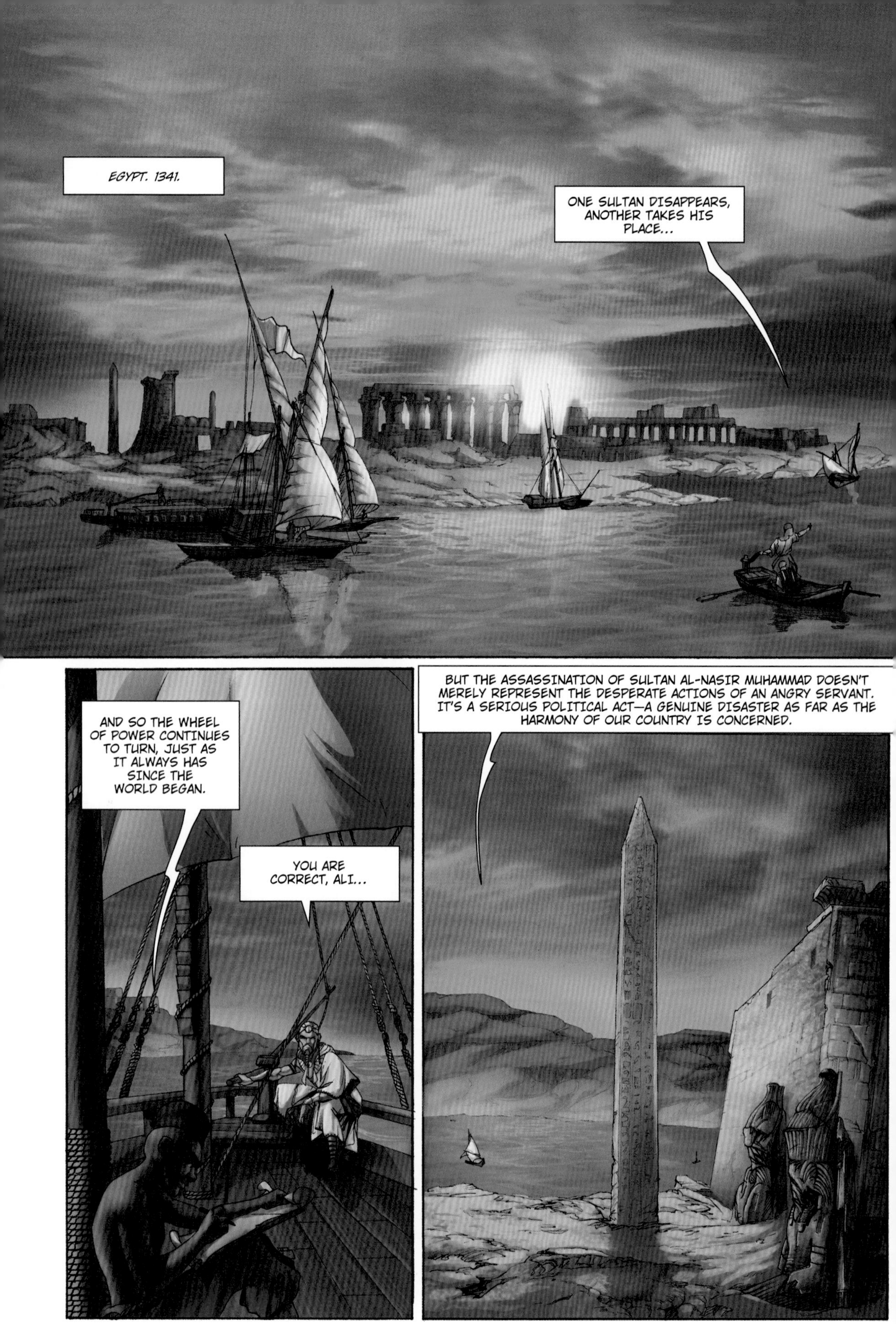
EGYPT. 1341.
ONE SULTAN DISAPPEARS, ANOTHER TAKES HIS PLACE...
AND SO THE WHEEL OF POWER CONTINUES TO TURN, JUST AS IT ALWAYS HAS SINCE THE WORLD BEGAN.
YOU ARE CORRECT, ALI...
BUT THE ASSASSINATION OF SULTAN AL-NASIR MUHAMMAD DOESN'T MERELY REPRESENT THE DESPERATE ACTIONS OF AN ANGRY SERVANT. IT'S A SERIOUS POLITICAL ACT—A GENUINE DISASTER AS FAR AS THE HARMONY OF OUR COUNTRY IS CONCERNED.

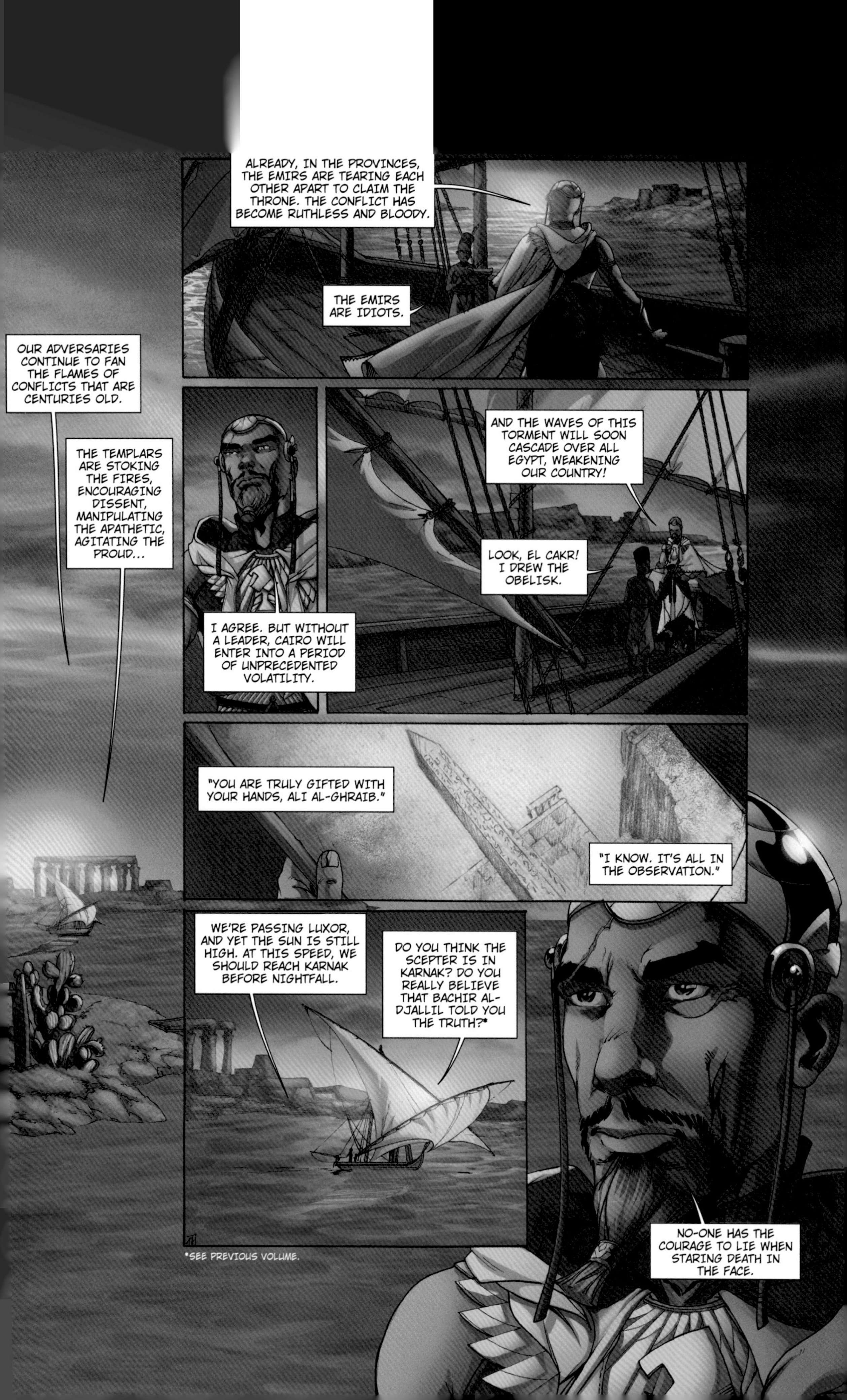
ALREADY, IN THE PROVINCES, THE EMIRS ARE TEARING EACH OTHER APART TO CLAIM THE THRONE. THE CONFLICT HAS BECOME RUTHLESS AND BLOODY.
THE EMIRS ARE IDIOTS.
OUR ADVERSARIES CONTINUE TO FAN THE FLAMES OF CONFLICTS THAT ARE CENTURIES OLD.
THE TEMPLARS ARE STOKING THE FIRES, ENCOURAGING DISSENT, MANIPULATING THE APATHETIC, AGITATING THE PROUD...
I AGREE. BUT WITHOUT A LEADER, CAIRO WILL ENTER INTO A PERIOD OF UNPRECEDENTED VOLATILITY.
AND THE WAVES OF THIS TORMENT WILL SOON CASCADE OVER ALL EGYPT, WEAKENING OUR COUNTRY!
LOOK, EL CAKR! I DREW THE OBELISK.
"YOU ARE TRULY GIFTED WITH YOUR HANDS, ALI AL-GHRAIB."
"I KNOW. IT'S ALL IN THE OBSERVATION."
WE'RE PASSING LUXOR, AND YET THE SUN IS STILL HIGH. AT THIS SPEED, WE SHOULD REACH KARNAK BEFORE NIGHTFALL.
DO YOU THINK THE SCEPTER IS IN KARNAK? DO YOU REALLY BELIEVE THAT BACHIR AL-DJALLIL TOLD YOU THE TRUTH?*
NO-ONE HAS THE COURAGE TO LIE WHEN STARING DEATH IN THE FACE.
*SEE PREVIOUS VOLUME.

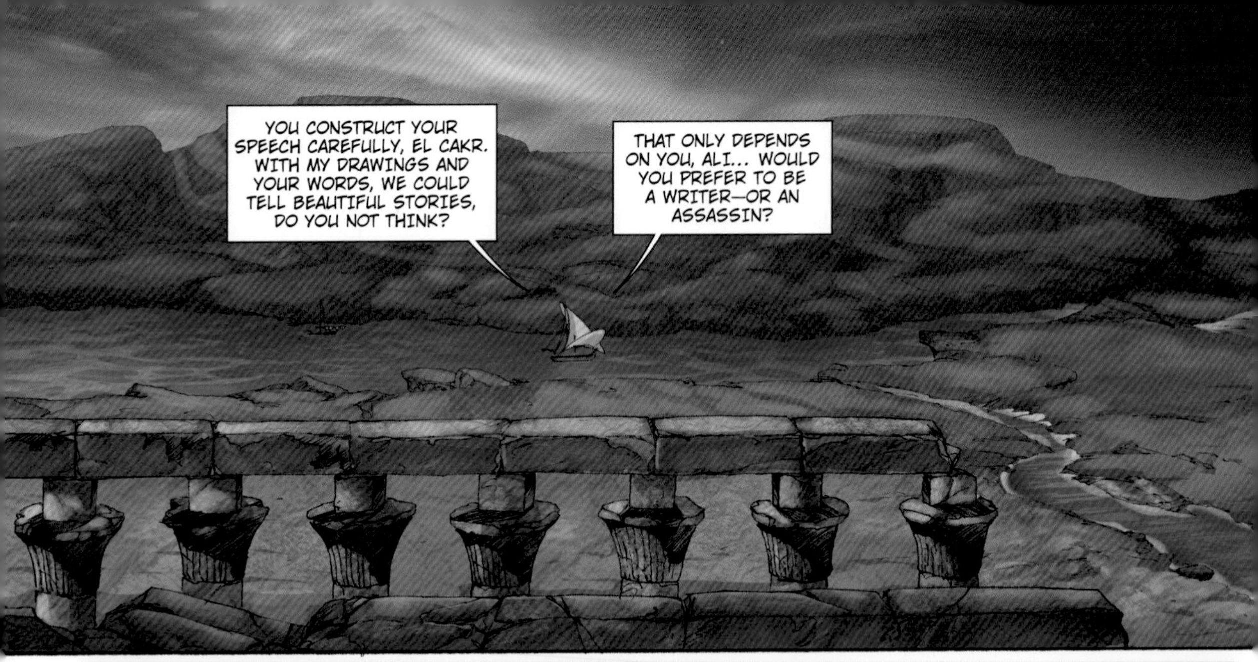
YOU CONSTRUCT YOUR SPEECH CAREFULLY, EL CAKR. WITH MY DRAWINGS AND YOUR WORDS, WE COULD TELL BEAUTIFUL STORIES, DO YOU NOT THINK?
THAT ONLY DEPENDS ON YOU, ALI... WOULD YOU PREFER TO BE A WRITER—OR AN ASSASSIN?

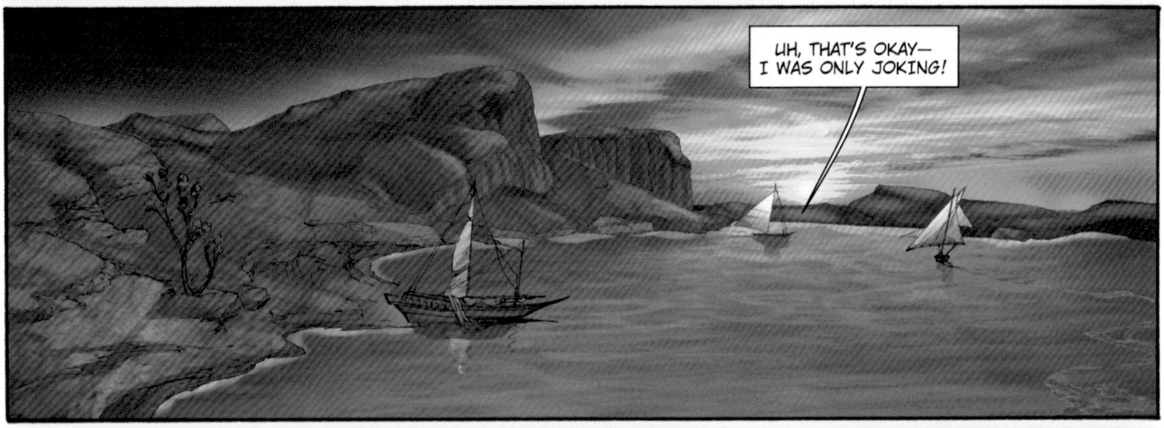
UH, THAT'S OKAY— I WAS ONLY JOKING!

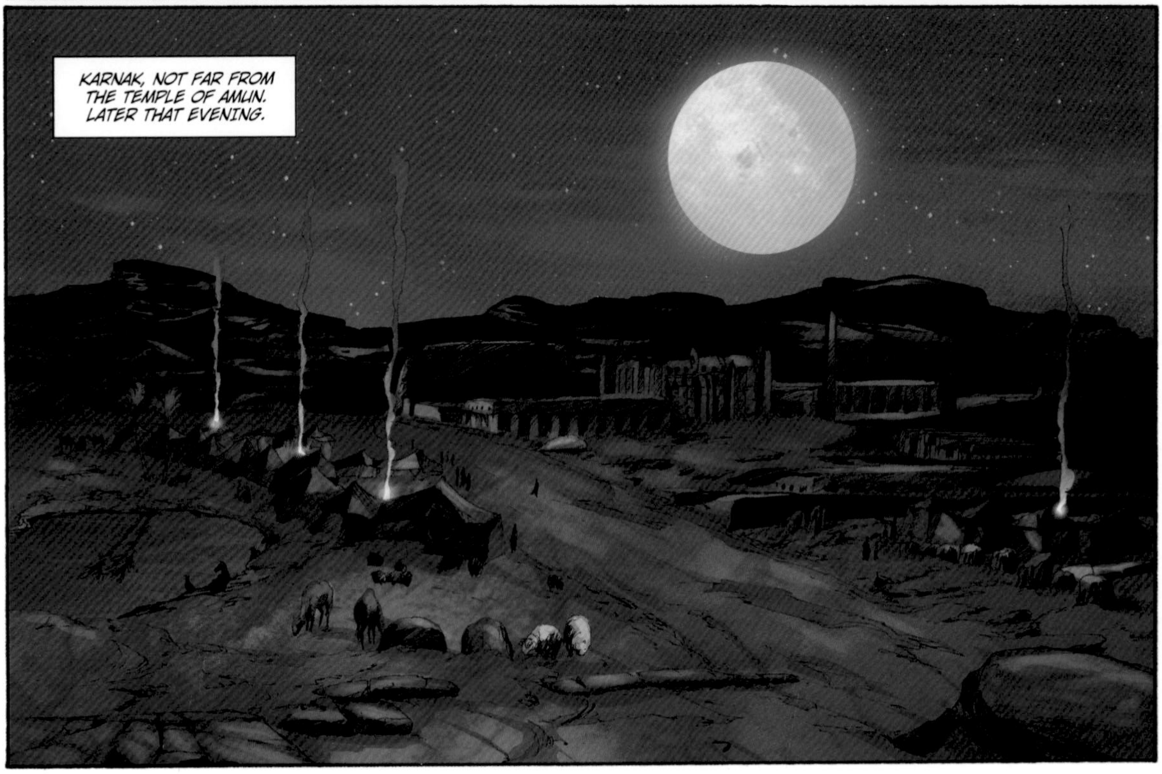
KARNAK, NOT FAR FROM THE TEMPLE OF AMUN. LATER THAT EVENING.

18

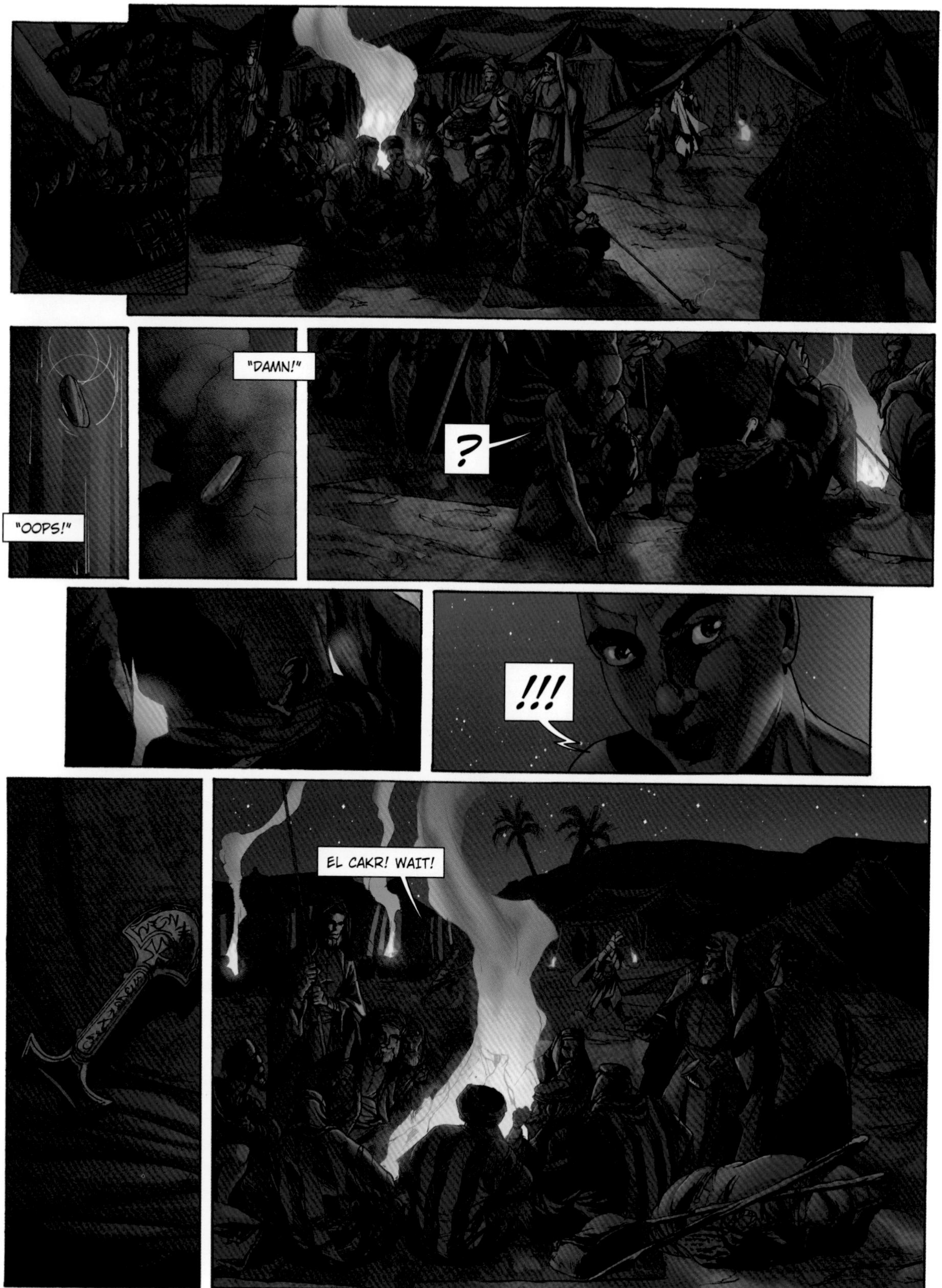
"OOPS!"
"DAMN!"
?
!!!
EL CAKR! WAIT!
19

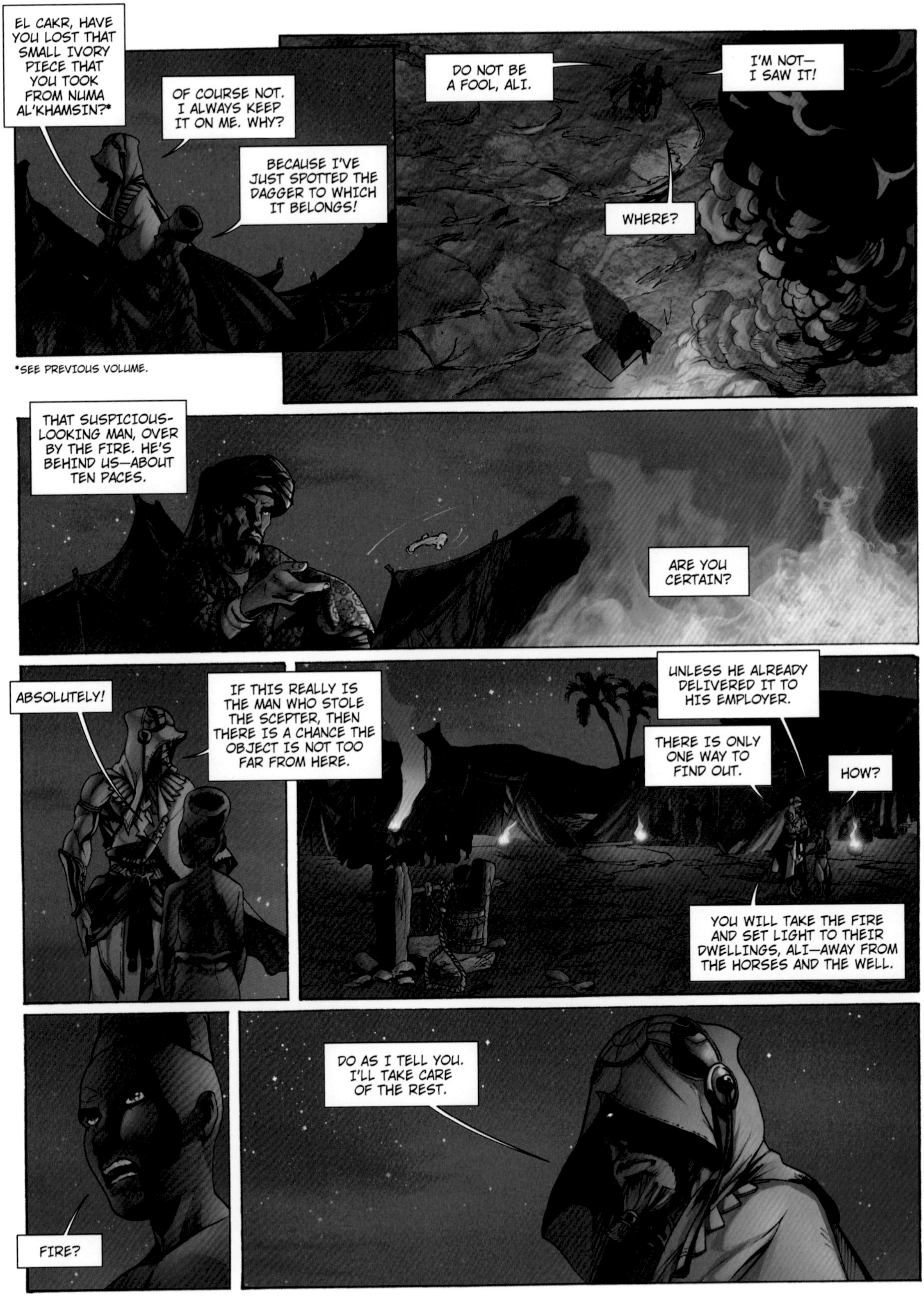
EL CAKR, HAVE YOU LOST THAT SMALL IVORY PIECE THAT YOU TOOK FROM NUMA AL'KHAMSIN?*
OF COURSE NOT. I ALWAYS KEEP IT ON ME. WHY?
BECAUSE I'VE JUST SPOTTED THE DAGGER TO WHICH IT BELONGS!
*SEE PREVIOUS VOLUME.
DO NOT BE A FOOL, ALI.
I'M NOT— I SAW IT!
WHERE?
THAT SUSPICIOUS-LOOKING MAN, OVER BY THE FIRE. HE'S BEHIND US—ABOUT TEN PACES.
ARE YOU CERTAIN?
ABSOLUTELY!
IF THIS REALLY IS THE MAN WHO STOLE THE SCEPTER, THEN THERE IS A CHANCE THE OBJECT IS NOT TOO FAR FROM HERE.
UNLESS HE ALREADY DELIVERED IT TO HIS EMPLOYER.
THERE IS ONLY ONE WAY TO FIND OUT.
HOW?
YOU WILL TAKE THE FIRE AND SET LIGHT TO THEIR DWELLINGS, ALI—AWAY FROM THE HORSES AND THE WELL.
FIRE?
DO AS I TELL YOU. I'LL TAKE CARE OF THE REST.

20

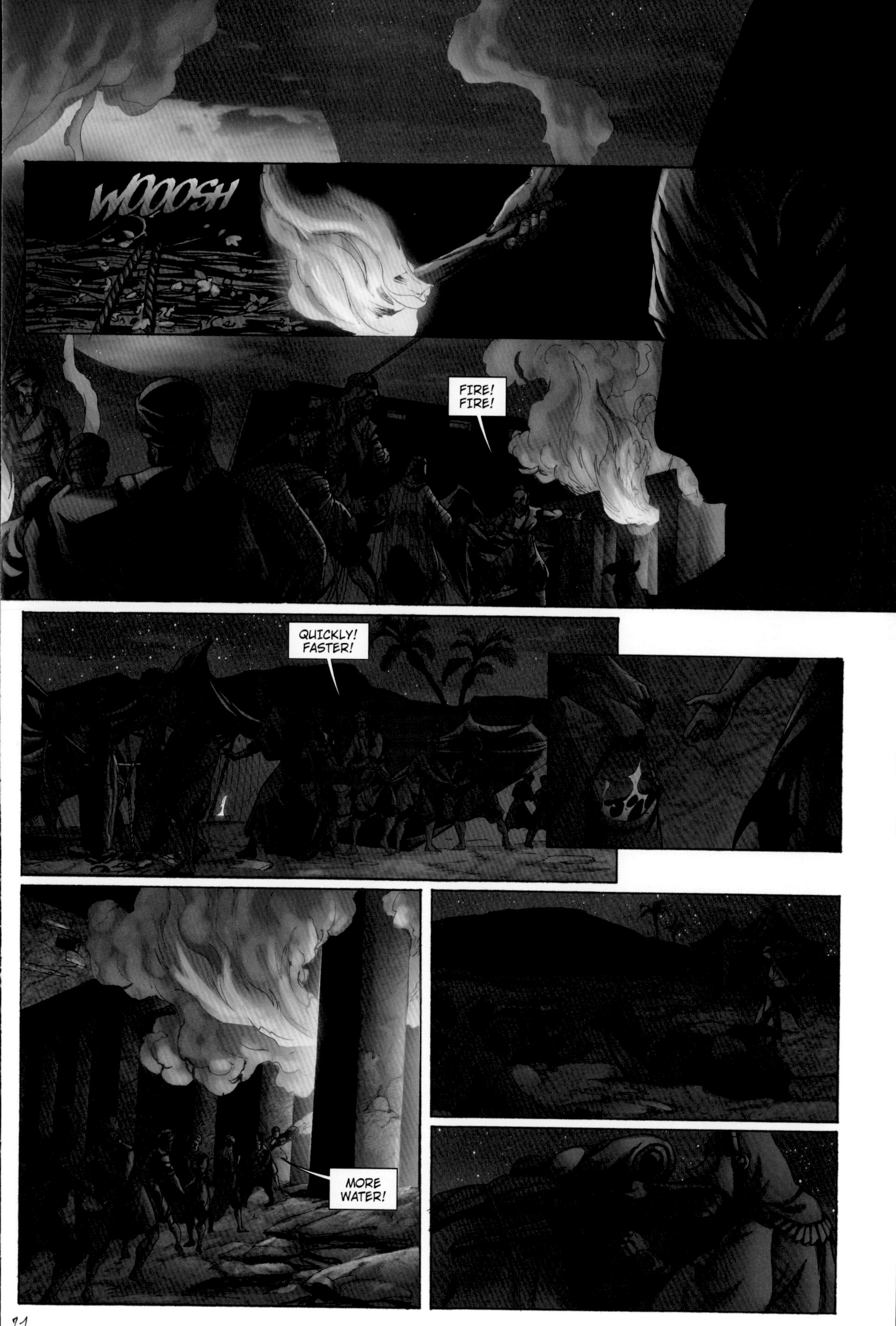
WOOOSH
FIRE! FIRE!
QUICKLY! FASTER!
MORE WATER!

21

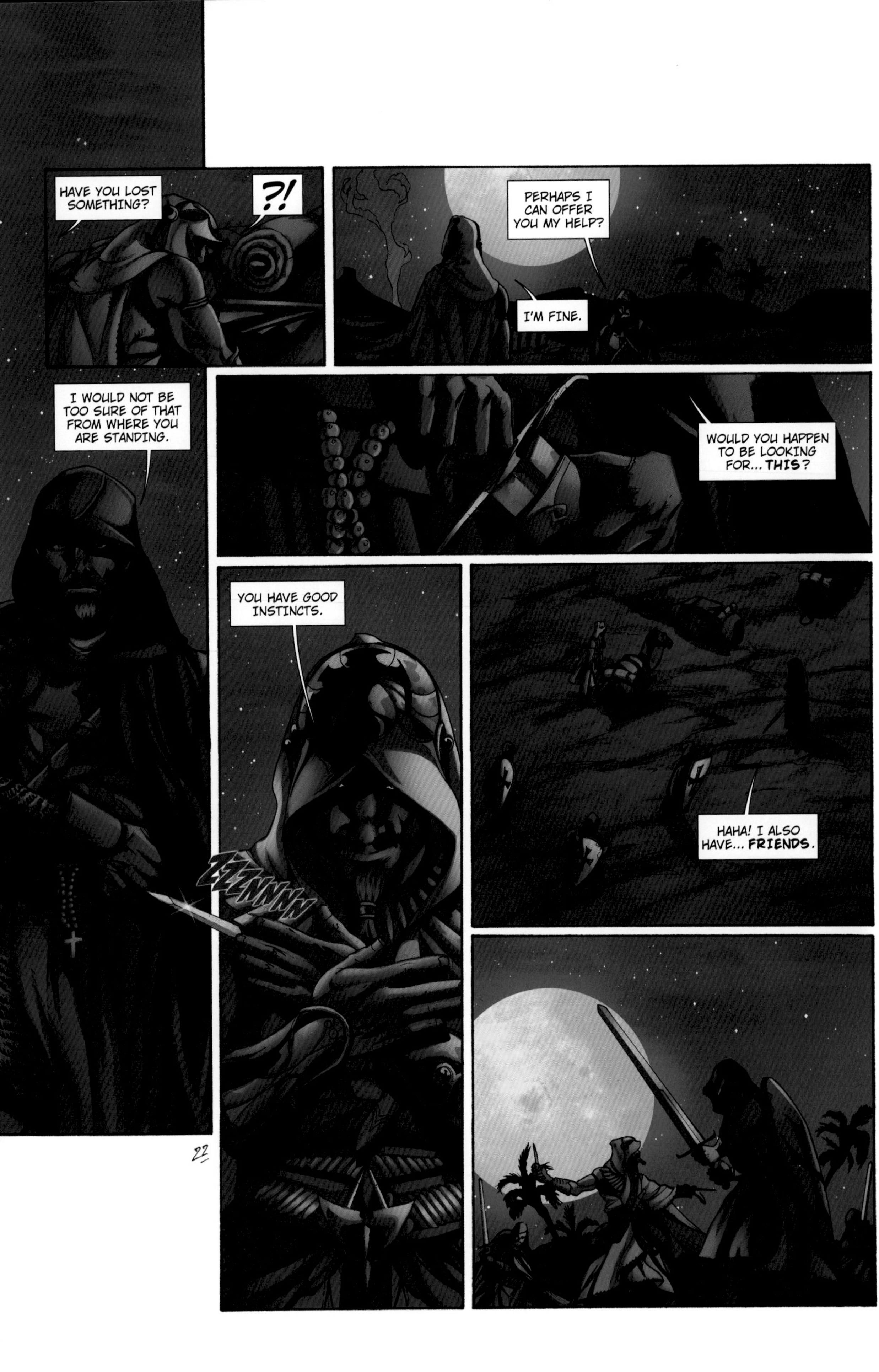
HAVE YOU LOST SOMETHING?
?!
PERHAPS I CAN OFFER YOU MY HELP?
I'M FINE.
I WOULD NOT BE TOO SURE OF THAT FROM WHERE YOU ARE STANDING.
WOULD YOU HAPPEN TO BE LOOKING FOR... **THIS**?
YOU HAVE GOOD INSTINCTS.
ZZZNNNN
HAHA! I ALSO HAVE... **FRIENDS**.

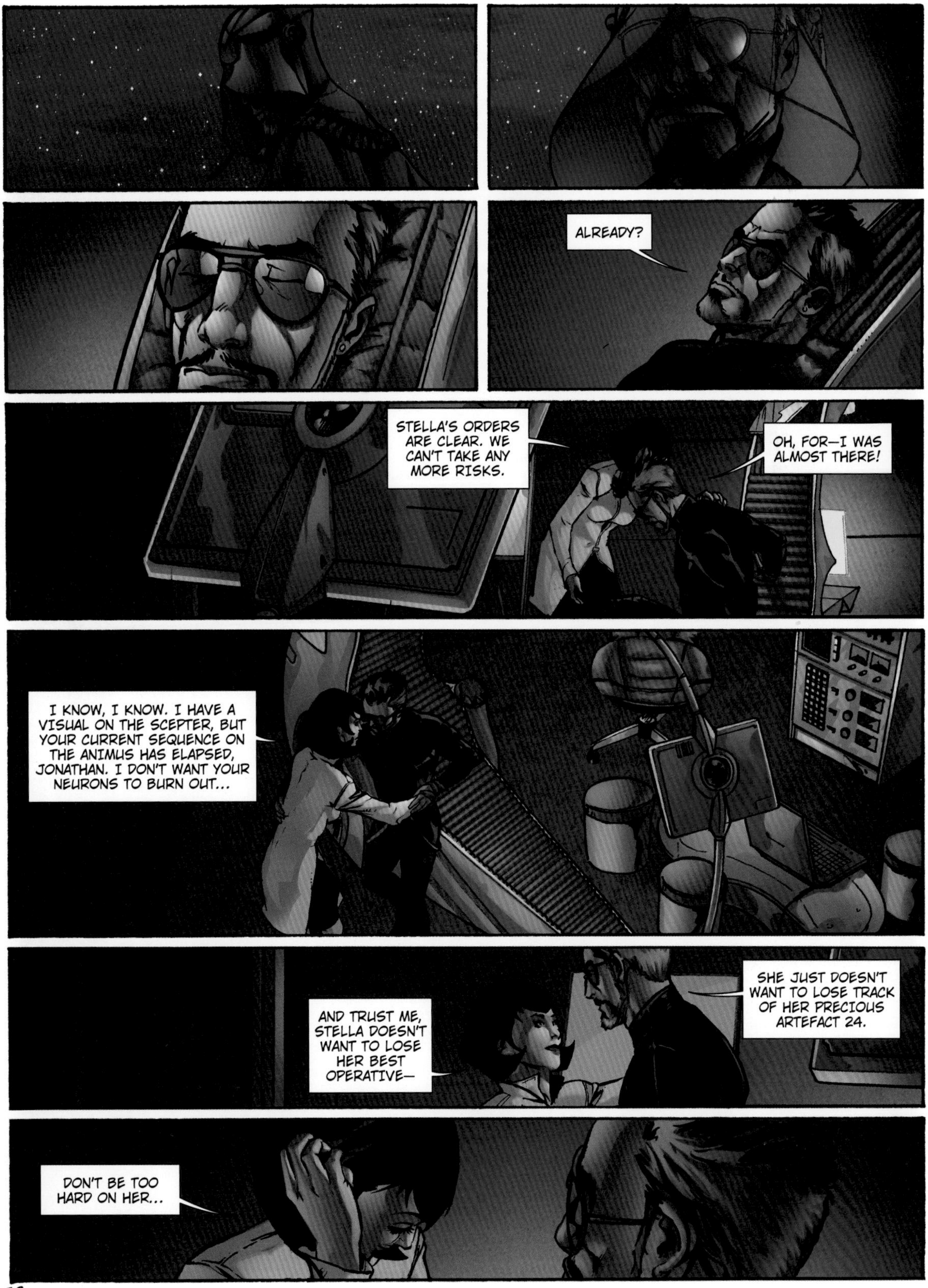
ALREADY?
STELLA'S ORDERS ARE CLEAR. WE CAN'T TAKE ANY MORE RISKS.
OH, FOR—I WAS ALMOST THERE!
I KNOW, I KNOW. I HAVE A VISUAL ON THE SCEPTER, BUT YOUR CURRENT SEQUENCE ON THE ANIMUS HAS ELAPSED, JONATHAN. I DON'T WANT YOUR NEURONS TO BURN OUT...
AND TRUST ME, STELLA DOESN'T WANT TO LOSE HER BEST OPERATIVE—
SHE JUST DOESN'T WANT TO LOSE TRACK OF HER PRECIOUS ARTEFACT 24.
DON'T BE TOO HARD ON HER...

23

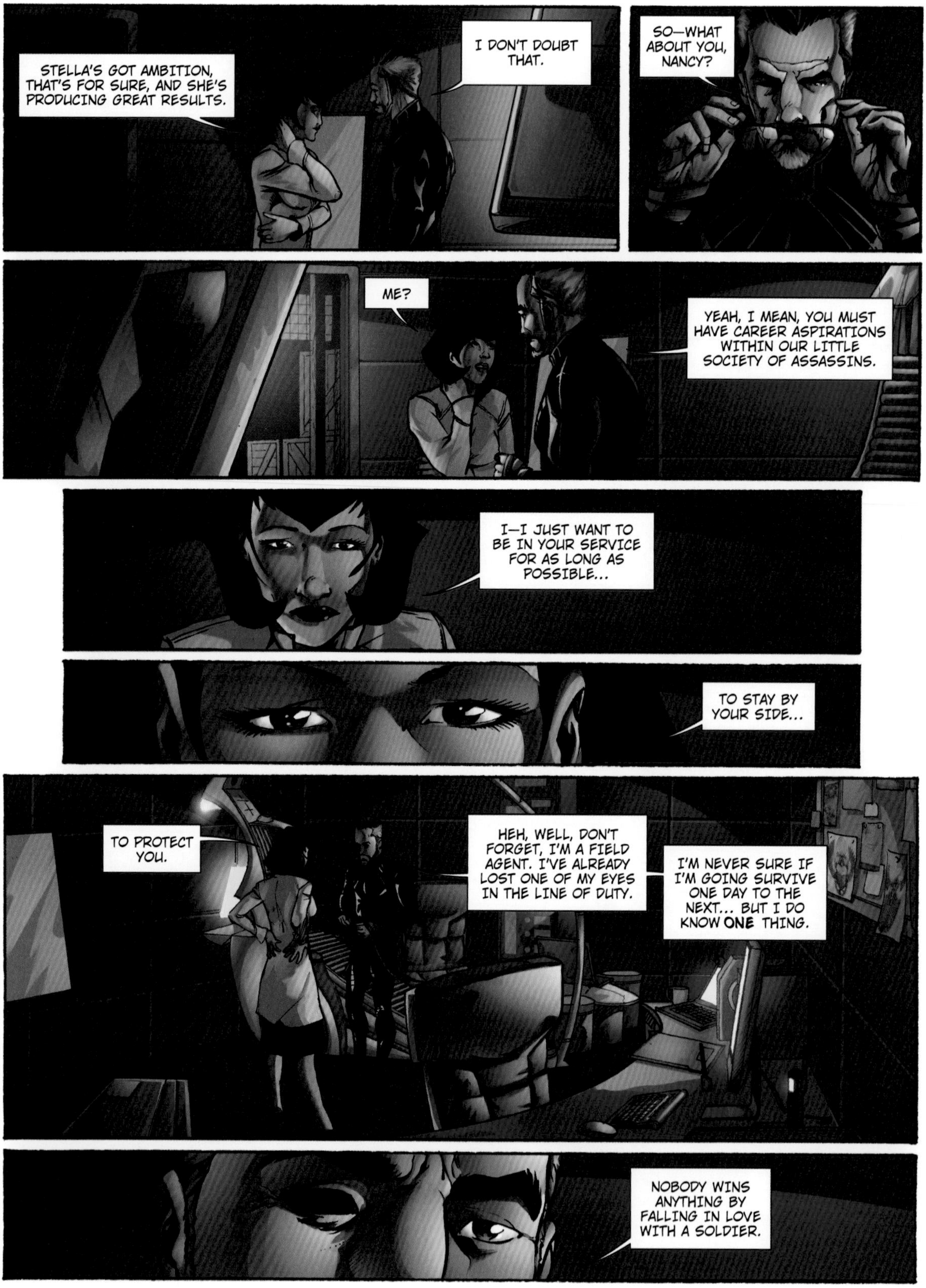
STELLA'S GOT AMBITION, THAT'S FOR SURE, AND SHE'S PRODUCING GREAT RESULTS.
I DON'T DOUBT THAT.
SO—WHAT ABOUT YOU, NANCY?
ME?
YEAH, I MEAN, YOU MUST HAVE CAREER ASPIRATIONS WITHIN OUR LITTLE SOCIETY OF ASSASSINS.
I—I JUST WANT TO BE IN YOUR SERVICE FOR AS LONG AS POSSIBLE...
TO STAY BY YOUR SIDE...
TO PROTECT YOU.
HEH, WELL, DON'T FORGET, I'M A FIELD AGENT. I'VE ALREADY LOST ONE OF MY EYES IN THE LINE OF DUTY.
I'M NEVER SURE IF I'M GOING SURVIVE ONE DAY TO THE NEXT... BUT I DO KNOW ONE THING.
NOBODY WINS ANYTHING BY FALLING IN LOVE WITH A SOLDIER.

24

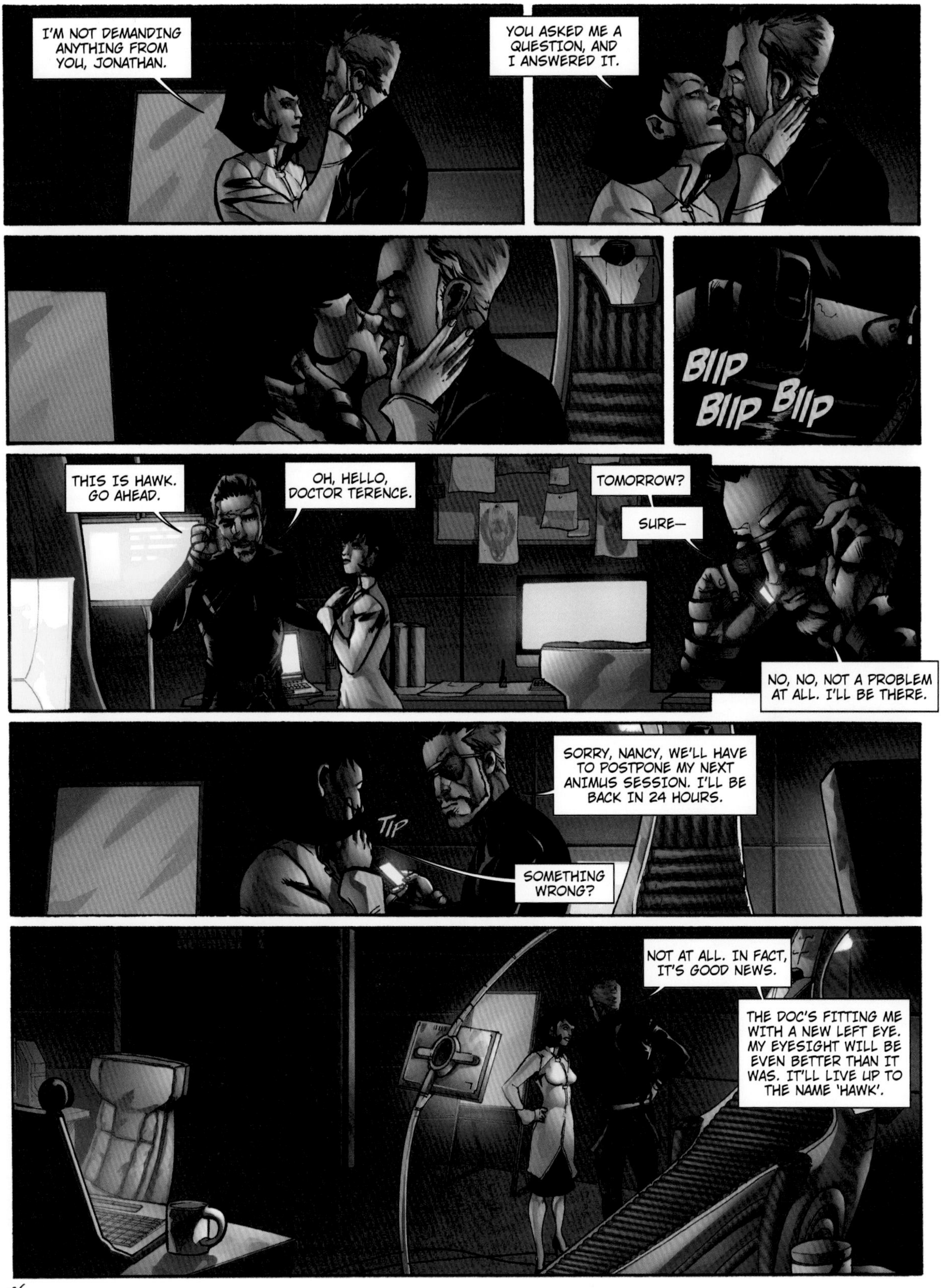
I'M NOT DEMANDING ANYTHING FROM YOU, JONATHAN.
YOU ASKED ME A QUESTION, AND I ANSWERED IT.
BIIP BIIP BIIP
THIS IS HAWK. GO AHEAD.
OH, HELLO, DOCTOR TERENCE.
TOMORROW?
SURE—
NO, NO, NOT A PROBLEM AT ALL. I'LL BE THERE.
SORRY, NANCY, WE'LL HAVE TO POSTPONE MY NEXT ANIMUS SESSION. I'LL BE BACK IN 24 HOURS.
TIP
SOMETHING WRONG?
NOT AT ALL. IN FACT, IT'S GOOD NEWS.
THE DOC'S FITTING ME WITH A NEW LEFT EYE. MY EYESIGHT WILL BE EVEN BETTER THAN IT WAS. IT'LL LIVE UP TO THE NAME 'HAWK'.

25,

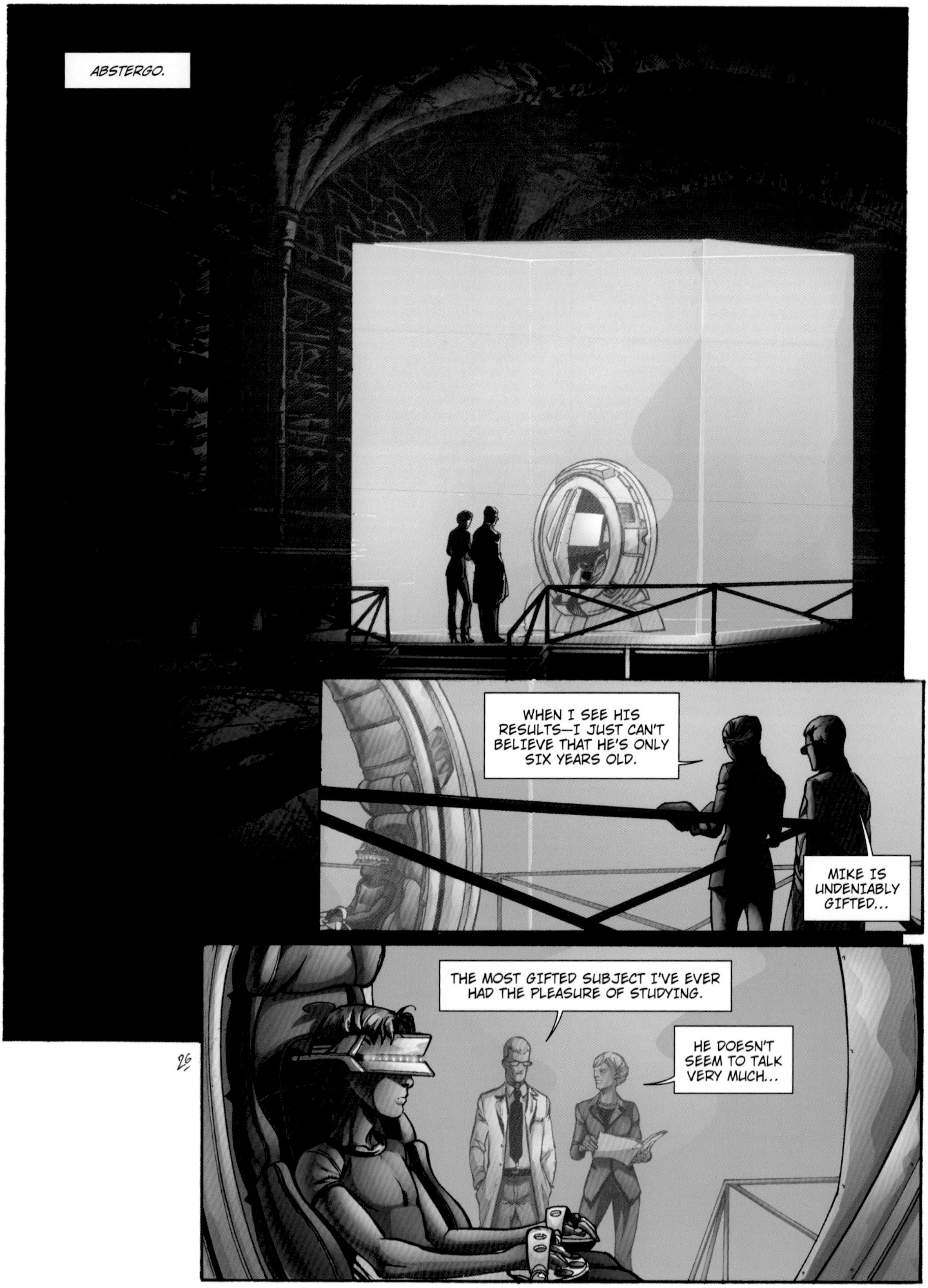
ABSTERGO.
WHEN I SEE HIS RESULTS—I JUST CAN'T BELIEVE THAT HE'S ONLY SIX YEARS OLD.
MIKE IS UNDENIABLY GIFTED...
THE MOST GIFTED SUBJECT I'VE EVER HAD THE PLEASURE OF STUDYING.
HE DOESN'T SEEM TO TALK VERY MUCH...

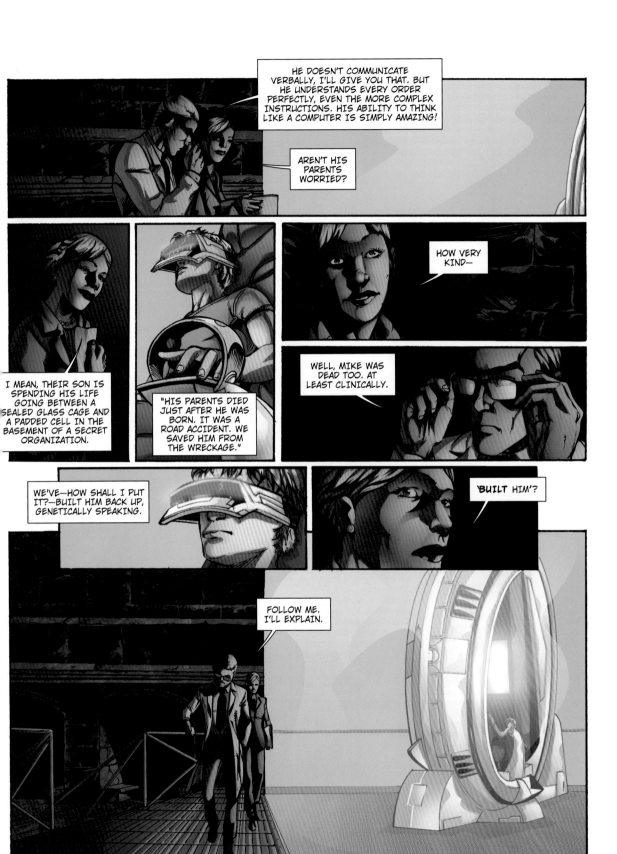

HE DOESN'T COMMUNICATE VERBALLY, I'LL GIVE YOU THAT. BUT HE UNDERSTANDS EVERY ORDER PERFECTLY, EVEN THE MORE COMPLEX INSTRUCTIONS. HIS ABILITY TO THINK LIKE A COMPUTER IS SIMPLY AMAZING!

AREN'T HIS PARENTS WORRIED?

HOW VERY KIND—

I MEAN, THEIR SON IS SPENDING HIS LIFE GOING BETWEEN A SEALED GLASS CAGE AND A PADDED CELL IN THE BASEMENT OF A SECRET ORGANIZATION.

"HIS PARENTS DIED JUST AFTER HE WAS BORN. IT WAS A ROAD ACCIDENT. WE SAVED HIM FROM THE WRECKAGE."

WELL, MIKE WAS DEAD TOO. AT LEAST CLINICALLY.

WE'VE—HOW SHALL I PUT IT?—BUILT HIM BACK UP, GENETICALLY SPEAKING.

'BUILT HIM'?

FOLLOW ME. I'LL EXPLAIN.

27

29

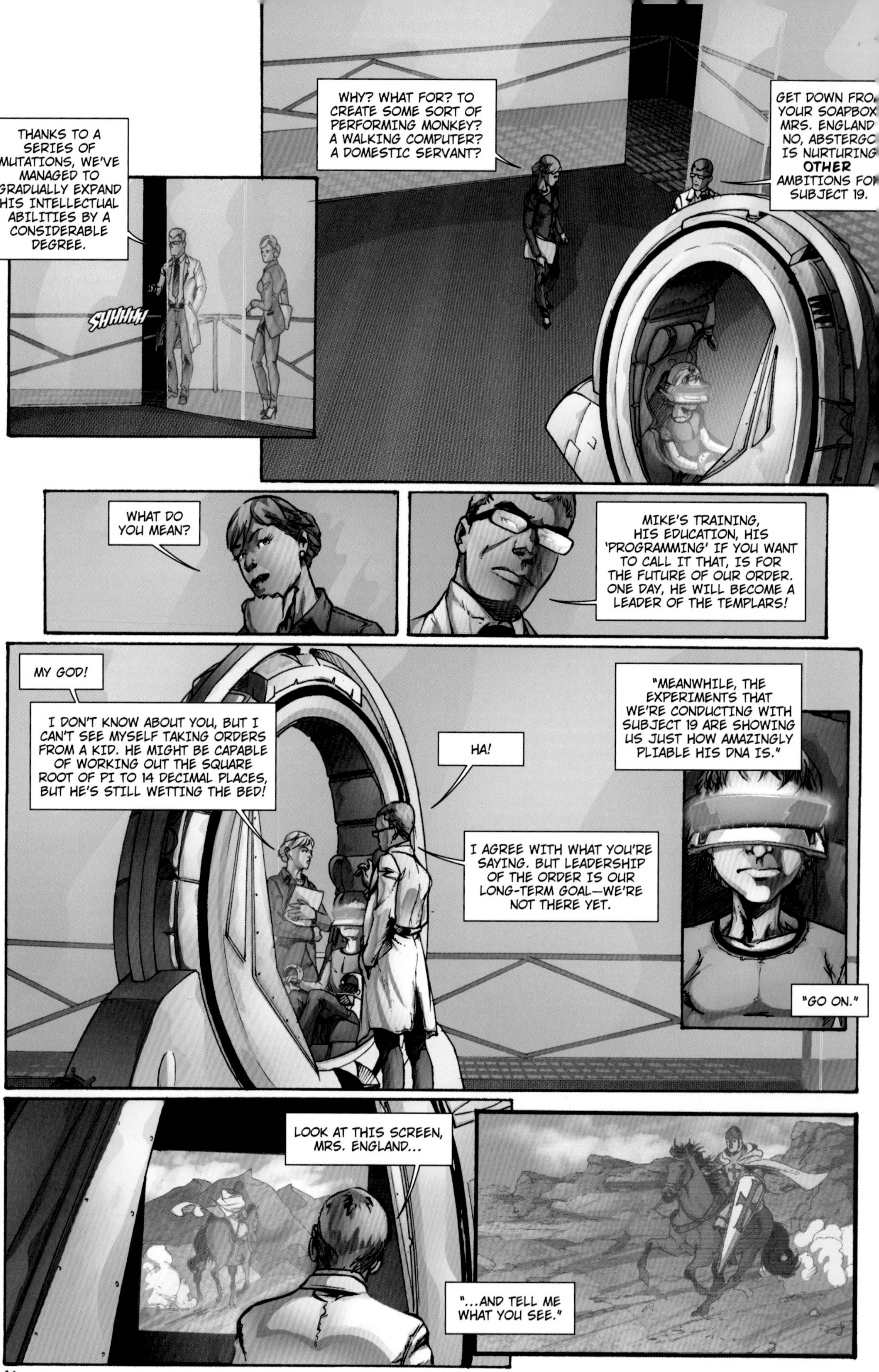
THANKS TO A SERIES OF MUTATIONS, WE'VE MANAGED TO GRADUALLY EXPAND HIS INTELLECTUAL ABILITIES BY A CONSIDERABLE DEGREE.
SHHHHH
WHY? WHAT FOR? TO CREATE SOME SORT OF PERFORMING MONKEY? A WALKING COMPUTER? A DOMESTIC SERVANT?
GET DOWN FRO YOUR SOAPBOX MRS. ENGLAND NO, ABSTERGO IS NURTURING OTHER AMBITIONS FO SUBJECT 19.
WHAT DO YOU MEAN?
MIKE'S TRAINING, HIS EDUCATION, HIS 'PROGRAMMING' IF YOU WANT TO CALL IT THAT, IS FOR THE FUTURE OF OUR ORDER. ONE DAY, HE WILL BECOME A LEADER OF THE TEMPLARS!
MY GOD!
I DON'T KNOW ABOUT YOU, BUT I CAN'T SEE MYSELF TAKING ORDERS FROM A KID. HE MIGHT BE CAPABLE OF WORKING OUT THE SQUARE ROOT OF PI TO 14 DECIMAL PLACES, BUT HE'S STILL WETTING THE BED!
HA!
I AGREE WITH WHAT YOU'RE SAYING. BUT LEADERSHIP OF THE ORDER IS OUR LONG-TERM GOAL—WE'RE NOT THERE YET.
"MEANWHILE, THE EXPERIMENTS THAT WE'RE CONDUCTING WITH SUBJECT 19 ARE SHOWING US JUST HOW AMAZINGLY PLIABLE HIS DNA IS."
"GO ON."
LOOK AT THIS SCREEN, MRS. ENGLAND...
"...AND TELL ME WHAT YOU SEE."

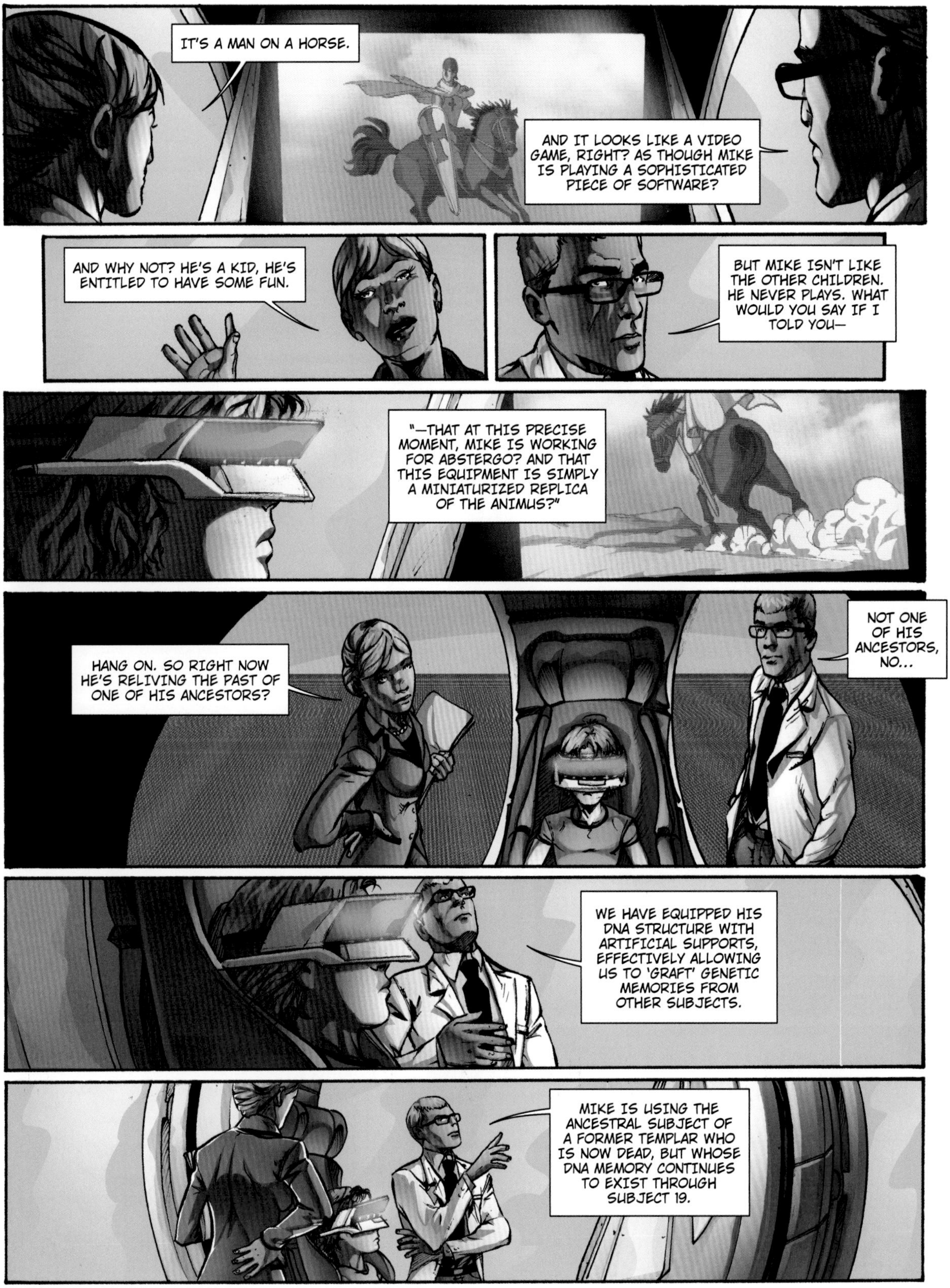
IT'S A MAN ON A HORSE.
AND IT LOOKS LIKE A VIDEO GAME, RIGHT? AS THOUGH MIKE IS PLAYING A SOPHISTICATED PIECE OF SOFTWARE?
AND WHY NOT? HE'S A KID, HE'S ENTITLED TO HAVE SOME FUN.
BUT MIKE ISN'T LIKE THE OTHER CHILDREN. HE NEVER PLAYS. WHAT WOULD YOU SAY IF I TOLD YOU—
"—THAT AT THIS PRECISE MOMENT, MIKE IS WORKING FOR ABSTERGO? AND THAT THIS EQUIPMENT IS SIMPLY A MINIATURIZED REPLICA OF THE ANIMUS?"
HANG ON. SO RIGHT NOW HE'S RELIVING THE PAST OF ONE OF HIS ANCESTORS?
NOT ONE OF HIS ANCESTORS, NO...
WE HAVE EQUIPPED HIS DNA STRUCTURE WITH ARTIFICIAL SUPPORTS, EFFECTIVELY ALLOWING US TO 'GRAFT' GENETIC MEMORIES FROM OTHER SUBJECTS.
MIKE IS USING THE ANCESTRAL SUBJECT OF A FORMER TEMPLAR WHO IS NOW DEAD, BUT WHOSE DNA MEMORY CONTINUES TO EXIST THROUGH SUBJECT 19.

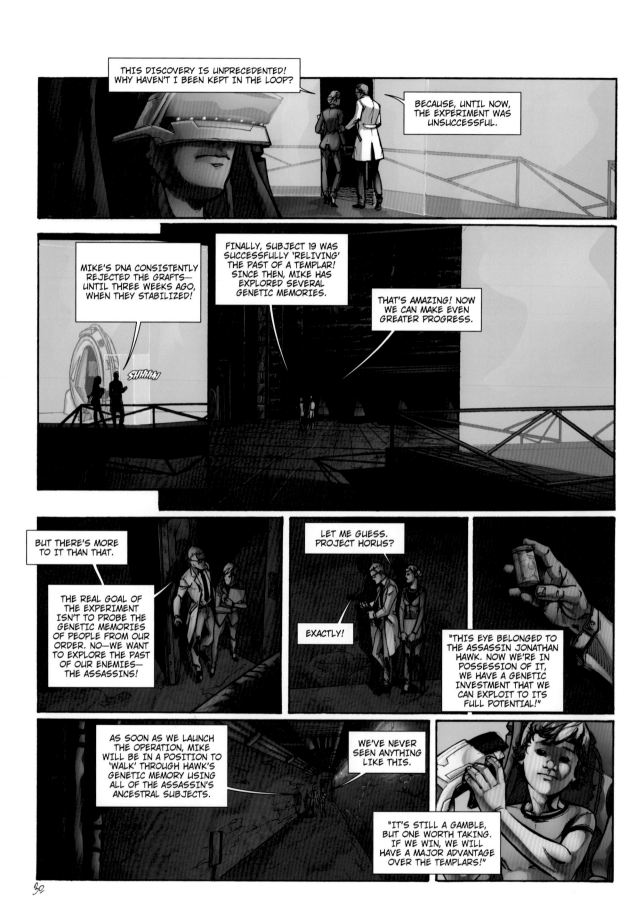

THIS DISCOVERY IS UNPRECEDENTED! WHY HAVEN'T I BEEN KEPT IN THE LOOP?

BECAUSE, UNTIL NOW, THE EXPERIMENT WAS UNSUCCESSFUL.

MIKE'S DNA CONSISTENTLY REJECTED THE GRAFTS— UNTIL THREE WEEKS AGO, WHEN THEY STABILIZED!

FINALLY, SUBJECT 19 WAS SUCCESSFULLY 'RELIVING' THE PAST OF A TEMPLAR! SINCE THEN, MIKE HAS EXPLORED SEVERAL GENETIC MEMORIES.

THAT'S AMAZING! NOW WE CAN MAKE EVEN GREATER PROGRESS.

SHHHH!

BUT THERE'S MORE TO IT THAN THAT.

THE REAL GOAL OF THE EXPERIMENT ISN'T TO PROBE THE GENETIC MEMORIES OF PEOPLE FROM OUR ORDER. NO—WE WANT TO EXPLORE THE PAST OF OUR ENEMIES— THE ASSASSINS!

LET ME GUESS. PROJECT HORUS?

EXACTLY!

"THIS EYE BELONGED TO THE ASSASSIN JONATHAN HAWK. NOW WE'RE IN POSSESSION OF IT, WE HAVE A GENETIC INVESTMENT THAT WE CAN EXPLOIT TO ITS FULL POTENTIAL!"

AS SOON AS WE LAUNCH THE OPERATION, MIKE WILL BE IN A POSITION TO 'WALK' THROUGH HAWK'S GENETIC MEMORY USING ALL OF THE ASSASSIN'S ANCESTRAL SUBJECTS.

WE'VE NEVER SEEN ANYTHING LIKE THIS.

"IT'S STILL A GAMBLE, BUT ONE WORTH TAKING. IF WE WIN, WE WILL HAVE A MAJOR ADVANTAGE OVER THE TEMPLARS!"

YOU CAN TAKE HIM THROUGH TO THE RECOVERY ROOM.

OF COURSE, DOCTOR.

IT'S DONE...

"INFORM ME WHEN HE WAKES UP."

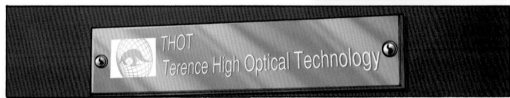

THOT
Terence High Optical Technology

HOW DO YOU FEEL, HAWK?

WOOZY...

THAT'S COMPLETELY NORMAL. HERE, TAKE THIS.

ANY HEADACHES?

NO... EVERYTHING'S FINE.

"WHAT IS—? I THOUGHT LOOKING LIKE A ROBOT WAS GONNA BE BAD ENOUGH, BUT A FREAKING PIRATE?!"

CALM DOWN, HAWK...

WHAT DO YOU THINK?

HONESTLY, DOC, I'VE LOOKED WORSE.

THANKS TO THE OPERATION, YOU'LL FIND THAT YOUR VISION WILL HAVE IMPROVED CONSIDERABLY.

ALL THE VISUAL INFORMATION THAT YOU RECEIVE WILL BE ANALYZED AND PROCESSED BEFOREHAND.

LIKE A RECORDING?

IN EFFECT. THERE WILL BE A SLIGHT DELAY, BUT IT SHOULDN'T EXCEED AROUND ONE-HUNDREDTH OF A SECOND.

YOUR VIEWPOINT WILL BE AUGMENTED CONSIDERABLY...

YOU WILL NEVER HAVE A PROBLEM SEEING IN COMPLETE AND TOTAL DARKNESS EVER AGAIN.

AND AS FOR EXTREME DISTANCES, YOU CAN ZOOM IN BY APPLYING PRESSURE ON THE SIDE.

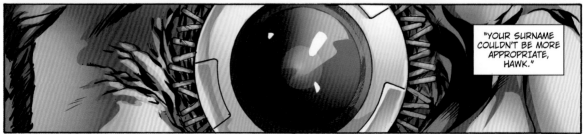

"YOUR SURNAME COULDN'T BE MORE APPROPRIATE, HAWK."

32

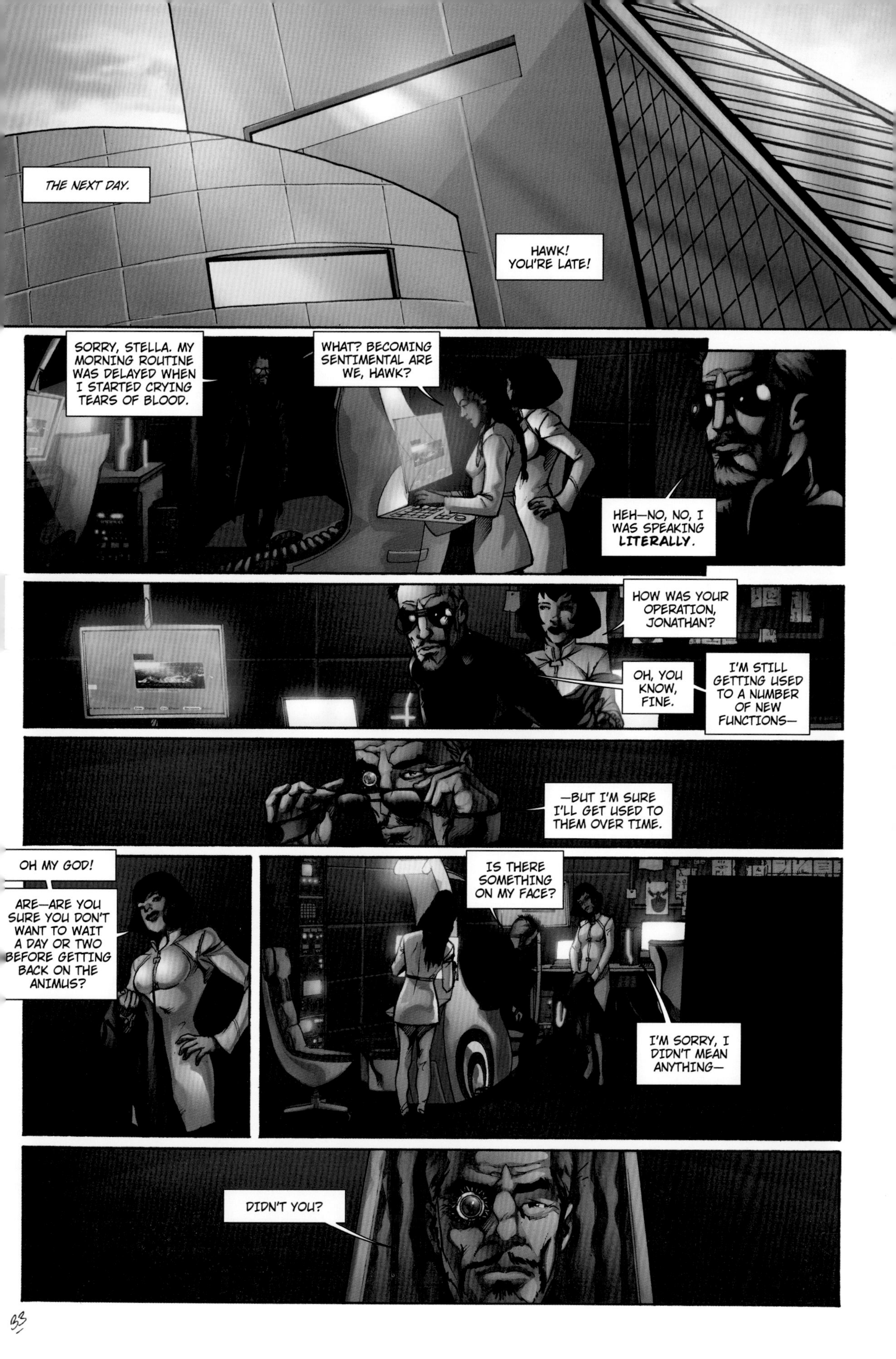
THE NEXT DAY.
HAWK! YOU'RE LATE!
SORRY, STELLA. MY MORNING ROUTINE WAS DELAYED WHEN I STARTED CRYING TEARS OF BLOOD.
WHAT? BECOMING SENTIMENTAL ARE WE, HAWK?
HEH—NO, NO, I WAS SPEAKING LITERALLY.
HOW WAS YOUR OPERATION, JONATHAN?
OH, YOU KNOW, FINE.
I'M STILL GETTING USED TO A NUMBER OF NEW FUNCTIONS—
—BUT I'M SURE I'LL GET USED TO THEM OVER TIME.
OH MY GOD!
ARE—ARE YOU SURE YOU DON'T WANT TO WAIT A DAY OR TWO BEFORE GETTING BACK ON THE ANIMUS?
IS THERE SOMETHING ON MY FACE?
I'M SORRY, I DIDN'T MEAN ANYTHING—
DIDN'T YOU?

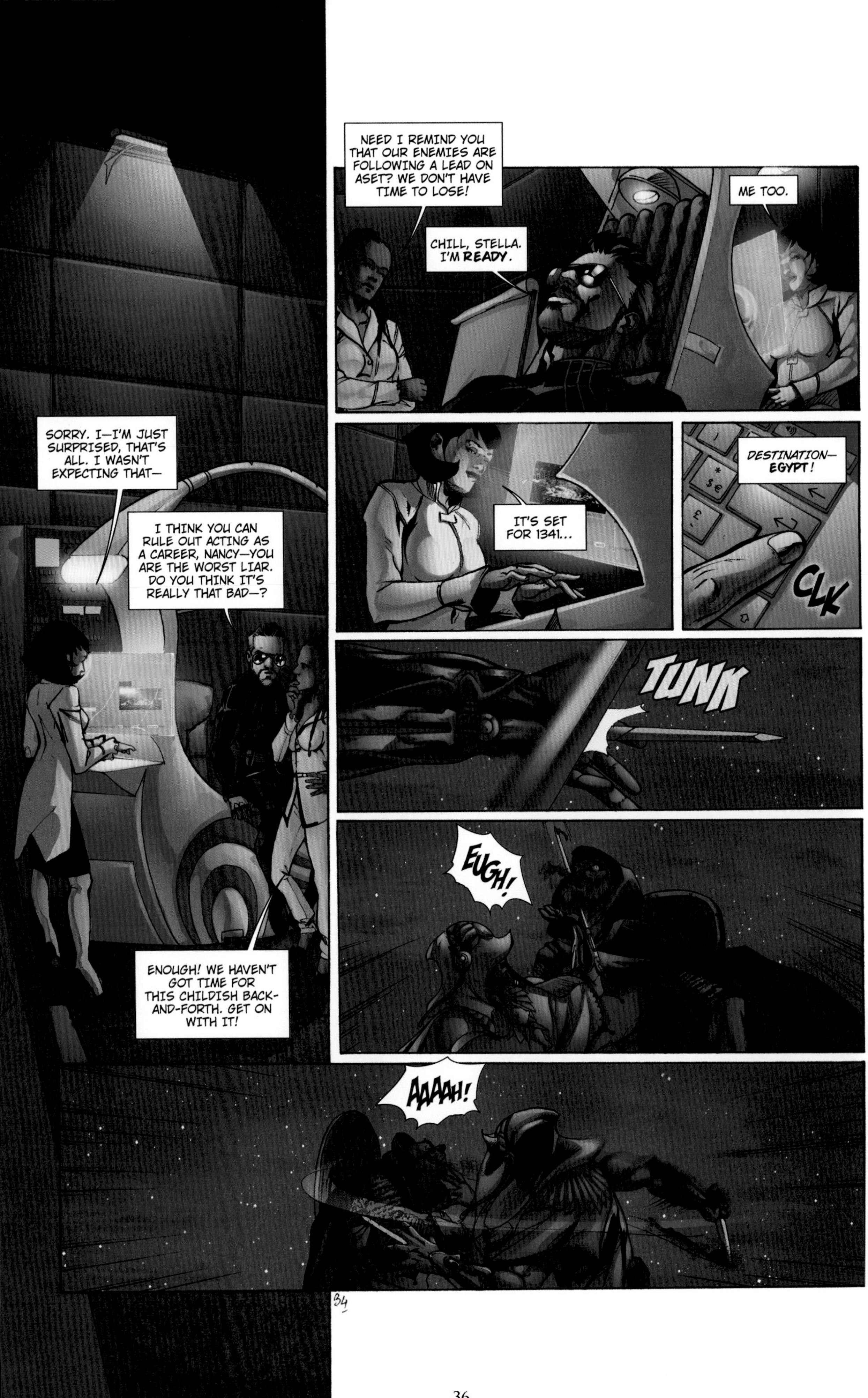

SORRY. I—I'M JUST SURPRISED, THAT'S ALL. I WASN'T EXPECTING THAT—
I THINK YOU CAN RULE OUT ACTING AS A CAREER, NANCY—YOU ARE THE WORST LIAR. DO YOU THINK IT'S REALLY THAT BAD—?
ENOUGH! WE HAVEN'T GOT TIME FOR THIS CHILDISH BACK-AND-FORTH. GET ON WITH IT!
NEED I REMIND YOU THAT OUR ENEMIES ARE FOLLOWING A LEAD ON ASET? WE DON'T HAVE TIME TO LOSE!
CHILL, STELLA. I'M **READY**.
ME TOO.
IT'S SET FOR 1341...
DESTINATION— **EGYPT**!
CLK
TUNK
EUGH!
AAAAH!
34

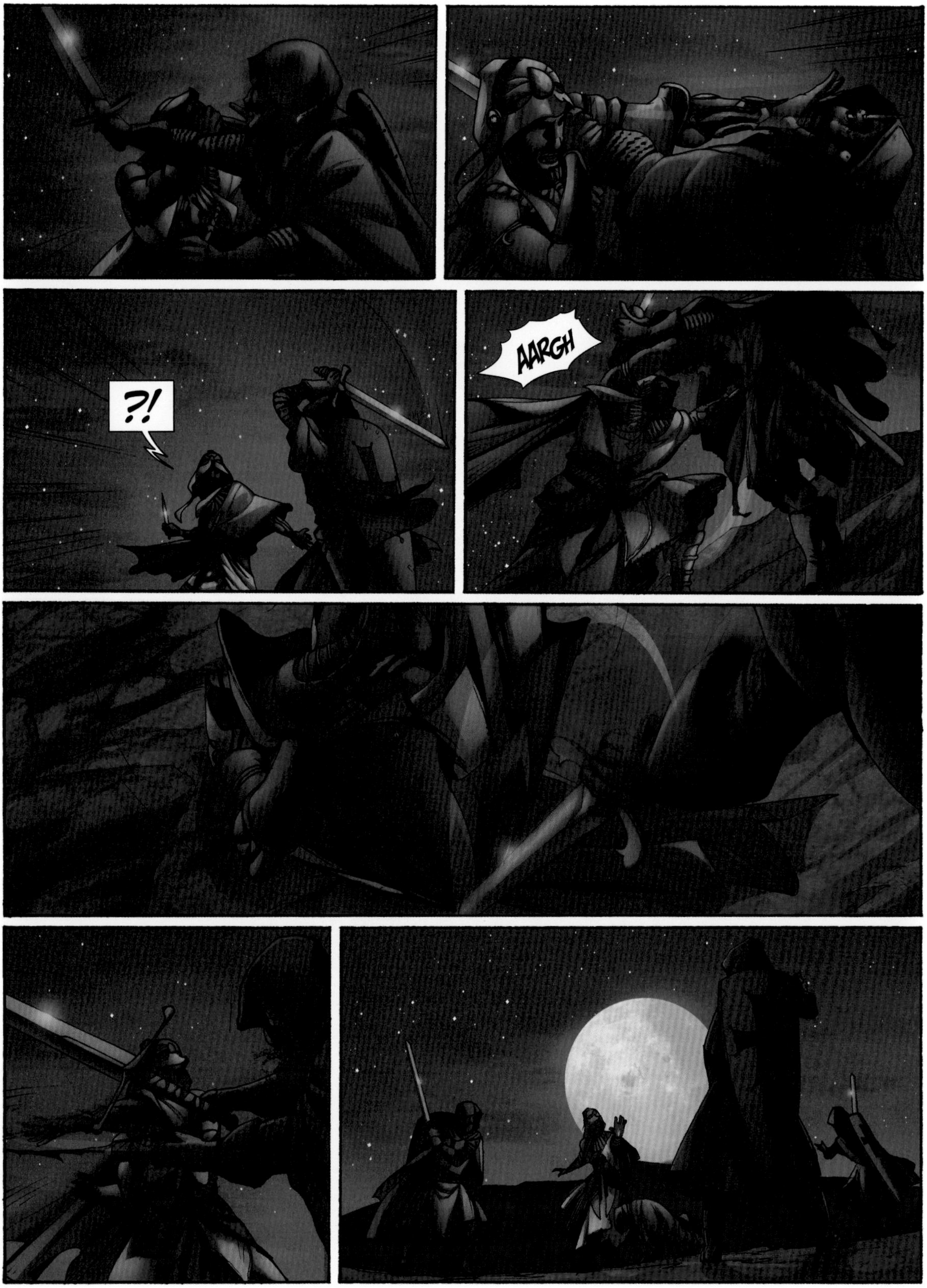
?!
AARGH

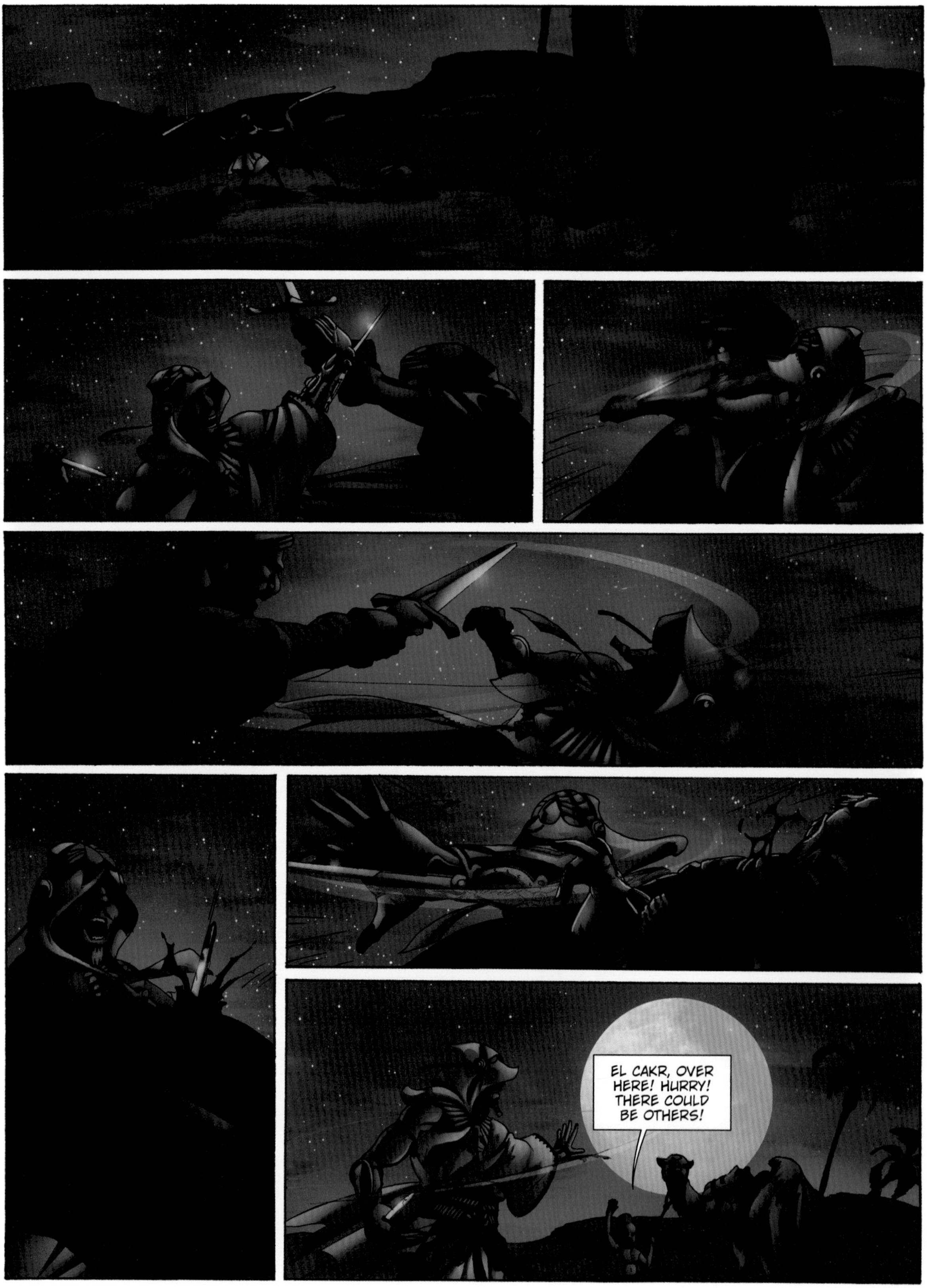
EL CAKR, OVER HERE! HURRY! THERE COULD BE OTHERS!

36

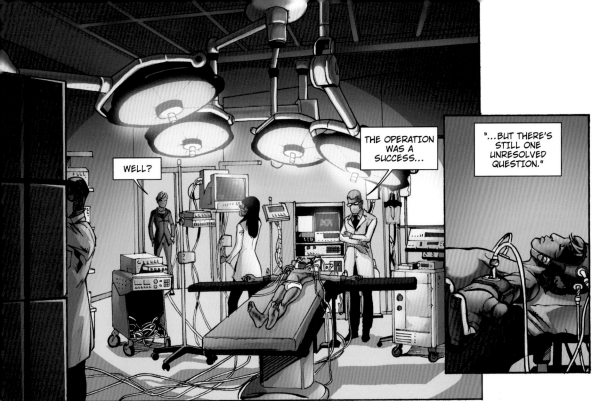

WELL?

THE OPERATION WAS A SUCCESS...

"...BUT THERE'S STILL ONE UNRESOLVED QUESTION."

WHAT?

WILL THE GRAFT **WORK**?

AND HOW LONG UNTIL WE KNOW FOR SURE?

VERY SOON. THIS MONITOR WILL TELL US...

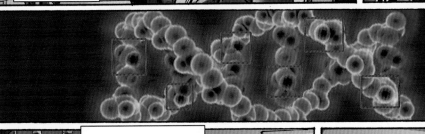

"USING ARTIFICIAL DYE, WE CAN TRACE THE ELEMENTS IMPRINTED ON HAWK'S DNA THAT WE HAVE ADDED TO MIKE'S LINEAGE. THEY'RE REPRESENTED BY THE RED ON THIS GRAPH."

AS SOON AS THESE COMPONENTS HAVE BEEN INTEGRATED, THEY WILL BECOME WHITE.

IN ROUGHLY 10 HOURS, WE'LL BE READY.

37

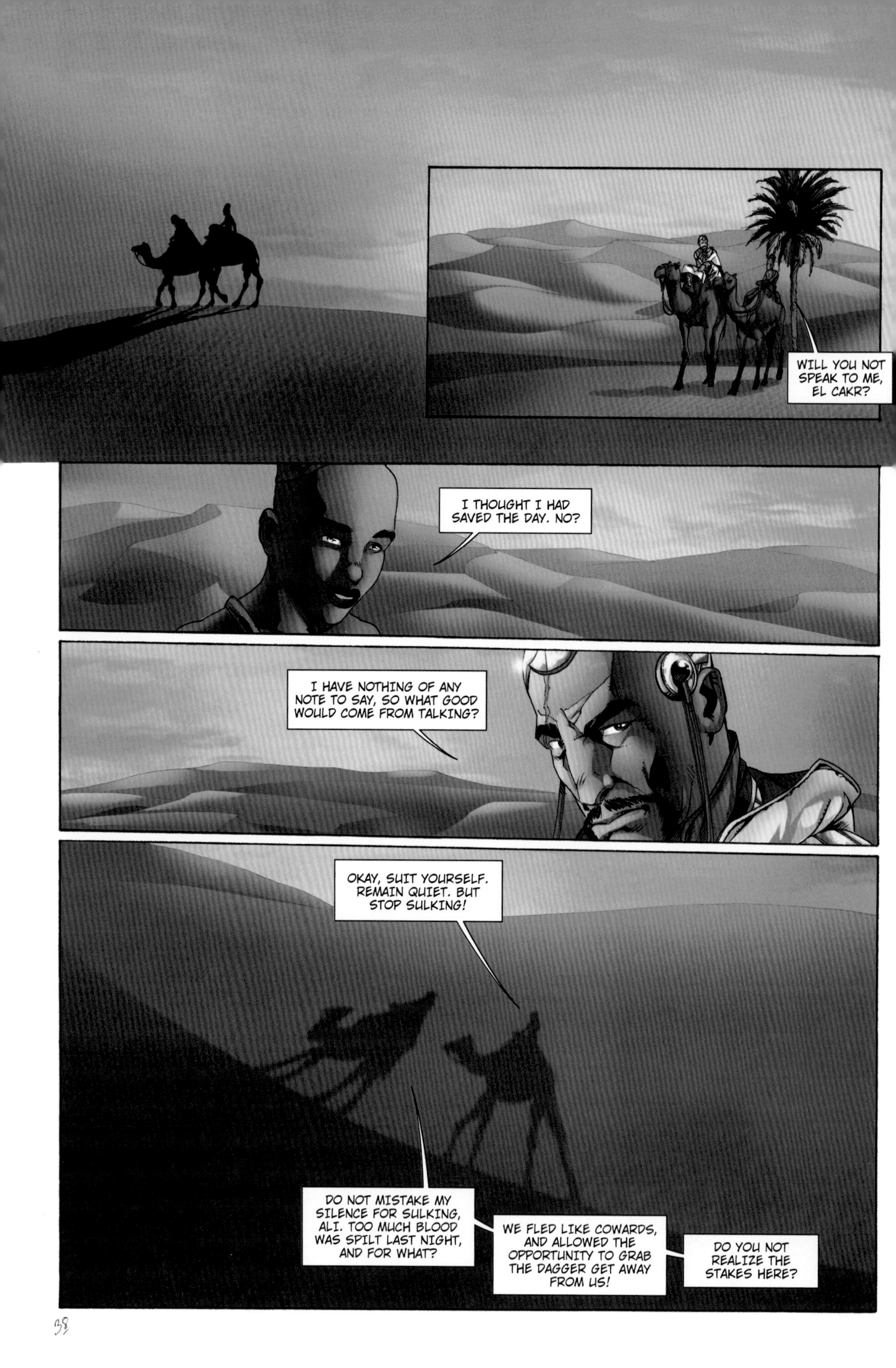
WILL YOU NOT SPEAK TO ME, EL CAKR?
I THOUGHT I HAD SAVED THE DAY. NO?
I HAVE NOTHING OF ANY NOTE TO SAY, SO WHAT GOOD WOULD COME FROM TALKING?
OKAY, SUIT YOURSELF. REMAIN QUIET. BUT STOP SULKING!
DO NOT MISTAKE MY SILENCE FOR SULKING, ALI. TOO MUCH BLOOD WAS SPILT LAST NIGHT, AND FOR WHAT?
WE FLED LIKE COWARDS, AND ALLOWED THE OPPORTUNITY TO GRAB THE DAGGER GET AWAY FROM US!
DO YOU NOT REALIZE THE STAKES HERE?

38

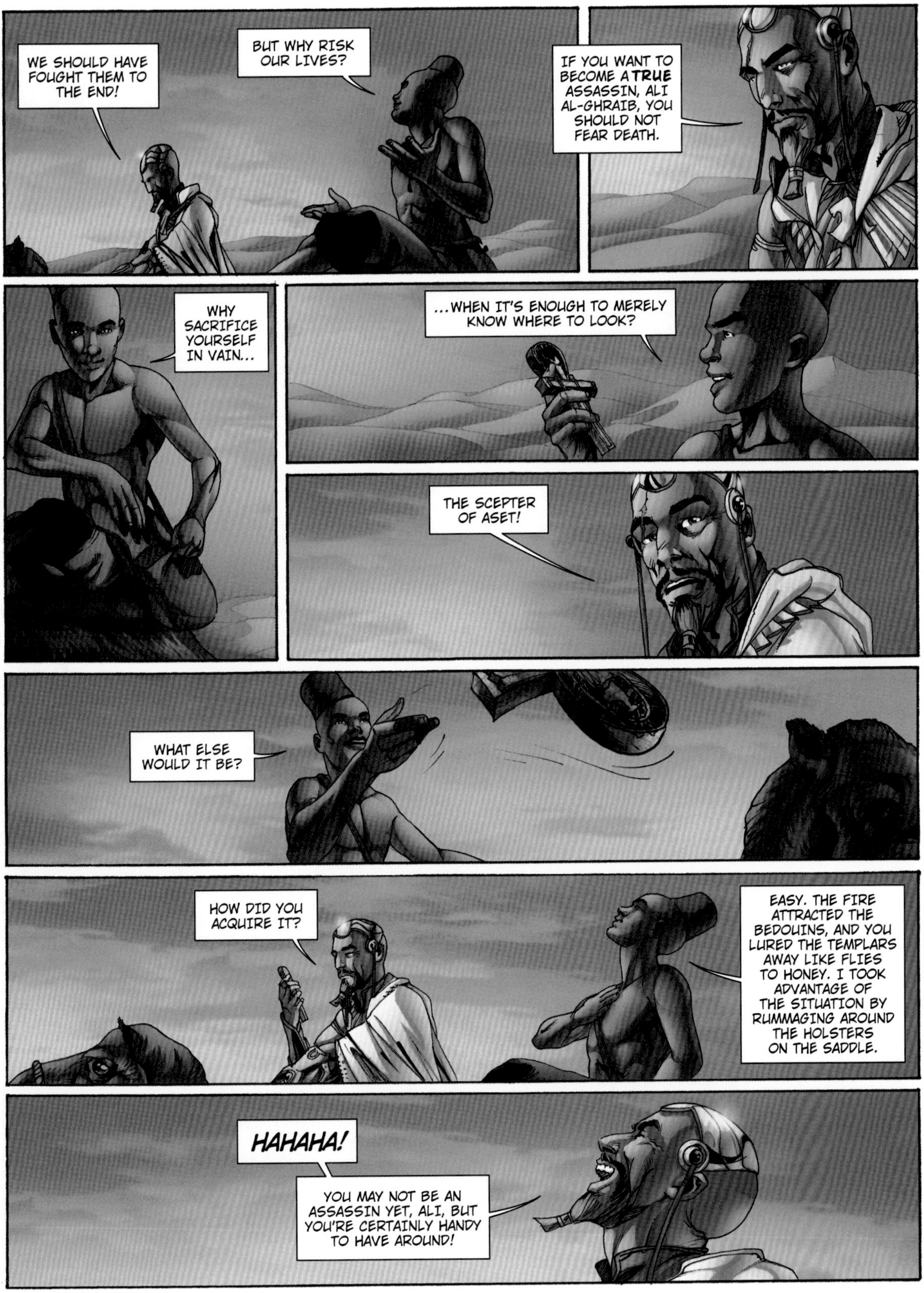
WE SHOULD HAVE FOUGHT THEM TO THE END!
BUT WHY RISK OUR LIVES?
IF YOU WANT TO BECOME A **TRUE** ASSASSIN, ALI AL-GHRAIB, YOU SHOULD NOT FEAR DEATH.
WHY SACRIFICE YOURSELF IN VAIN...
...WHEN IT'S ENOUGH TO MERELY KNOW WHERE TO LOOK?
THE SCEPTER OF ASET!
WHAT ELSE WOULD IT BE?
HOW DID YOU ACQUIRE IT?
EASY. THE FIRE ATTRACTED THE BEDOUINS, AND YOU LURED THE TEMPLARS AWAY LIKE FLIES TO HONEY. I TOOK ADVANTAGE OF THE SITUATION BY RUMMAGING AROUND THE HOLSTERS ON THE SADDLE.
HAHAHA!
YOU MAY NOT BE AN ASSASSIN YET, ALI, BUT YOU'RE CERTAINLY HANDY TO HAVE AROUND!
39

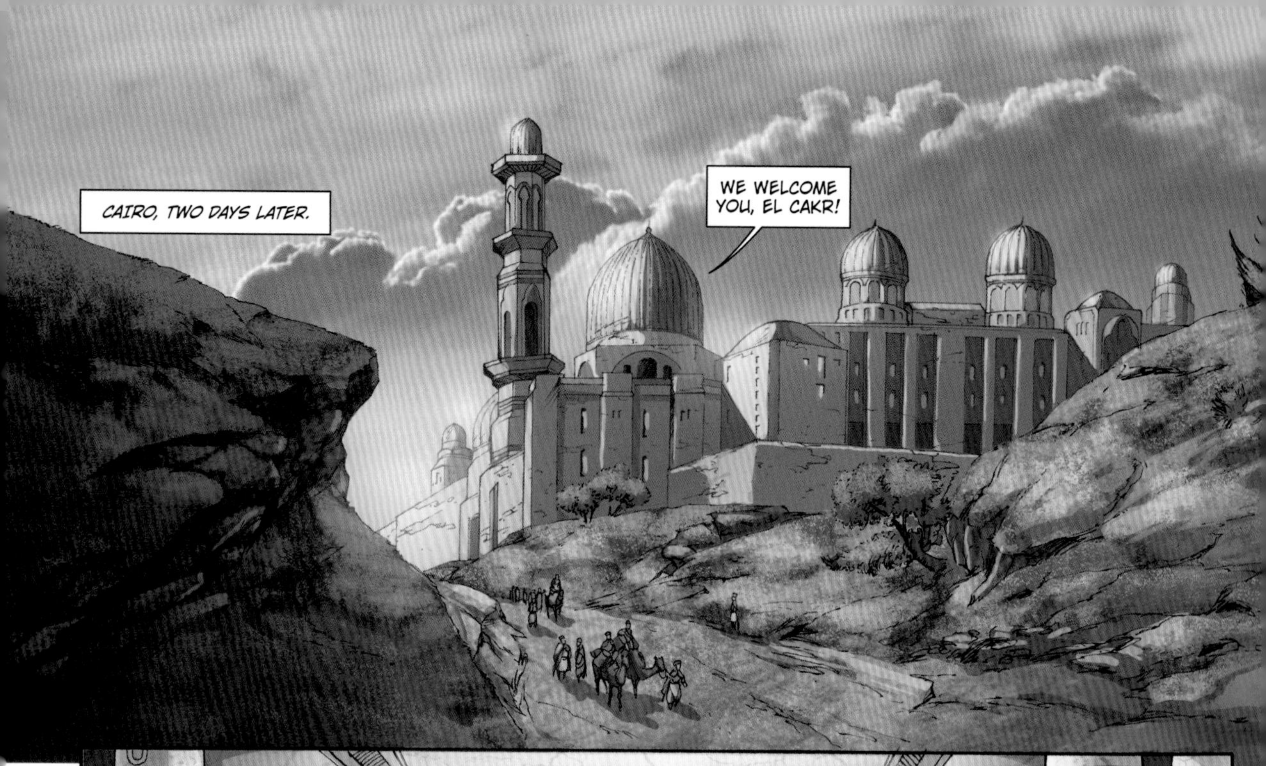
CAIRO, TWO DAYS LATER.
WE WELCOME YOU, EL CAKR!

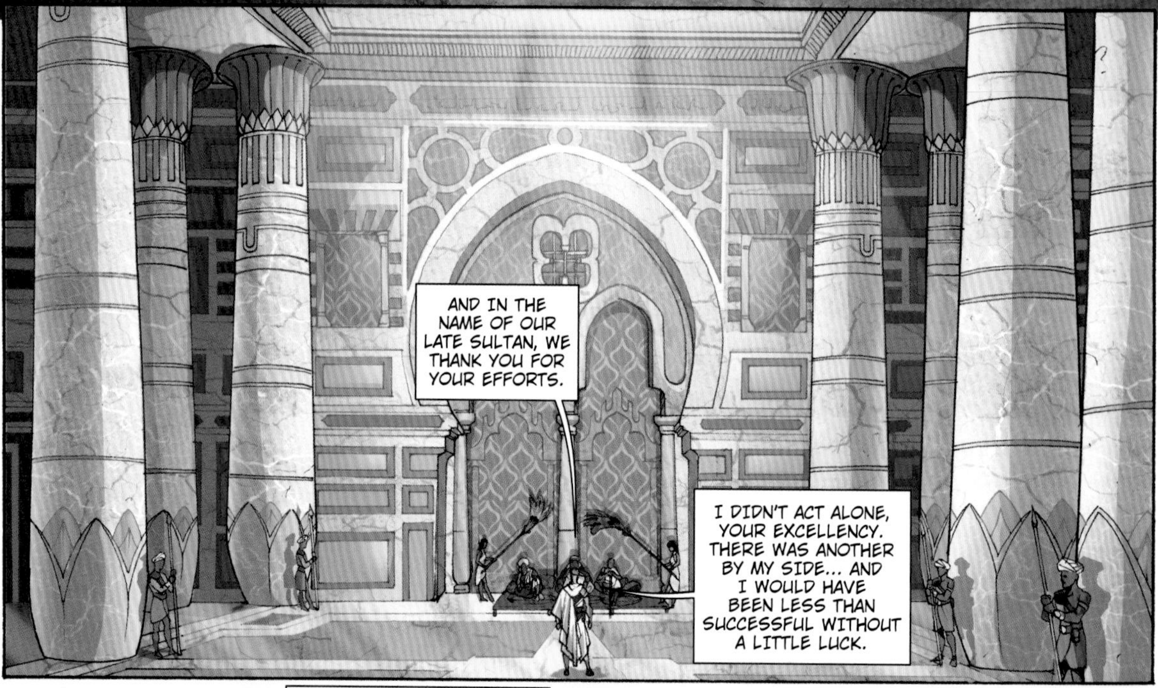
AND IN THE NAME OF OUR LATE SULTAN, WE THANK YOU FOR YOUR EFFORTS.
I DIDN'T ACT ALONE, YOUR EXCELLENCY. THERE WAS ANOTHER BY MY SIDE... AND I WOULD HAVE BEEN LESS THAN SUCCESSFUL WITHOUT A LITTLE LUCK.

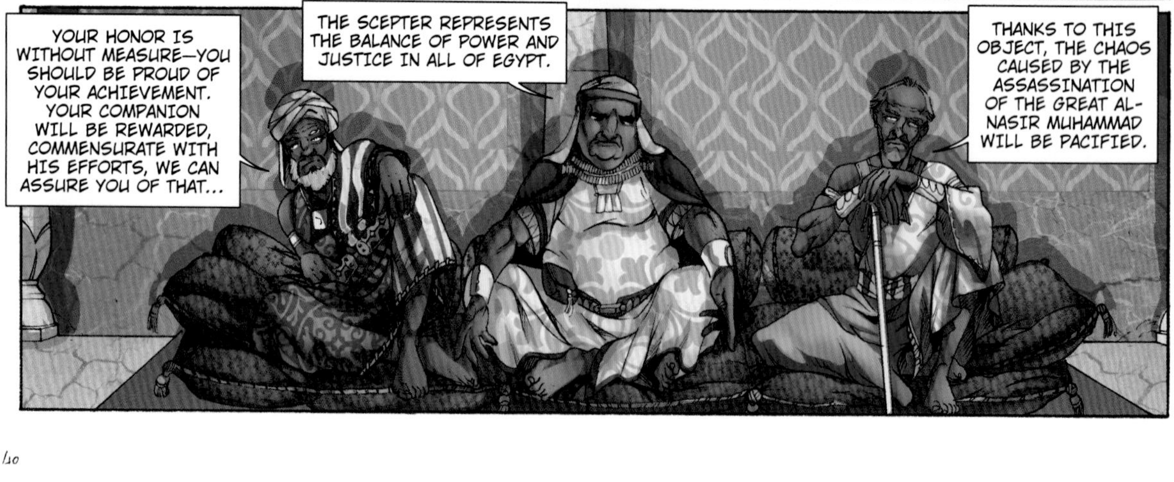
YOUR HONOR IS WITHOUT MEASURE—YOU SHOULD BE PROUD OF YOUR ACHIEVEMENT. YOUR COMPANION WILL BE REWARDED, COMMENSURATE WITH HIS EFFORTS, WE CAN ASSURE YOU OF THAT...
THE SCEPTER REPRESENTS THE BALANCE OF POWER AND JUSTICE IN ALL OF EGYPT.
THANKS TO THIS OBJECT, THE CHAOS CAUSED BY THE ASSASSINATION OF THE GREAT AL-NASIR MUHAMMAD WILL BE PACIFIED.

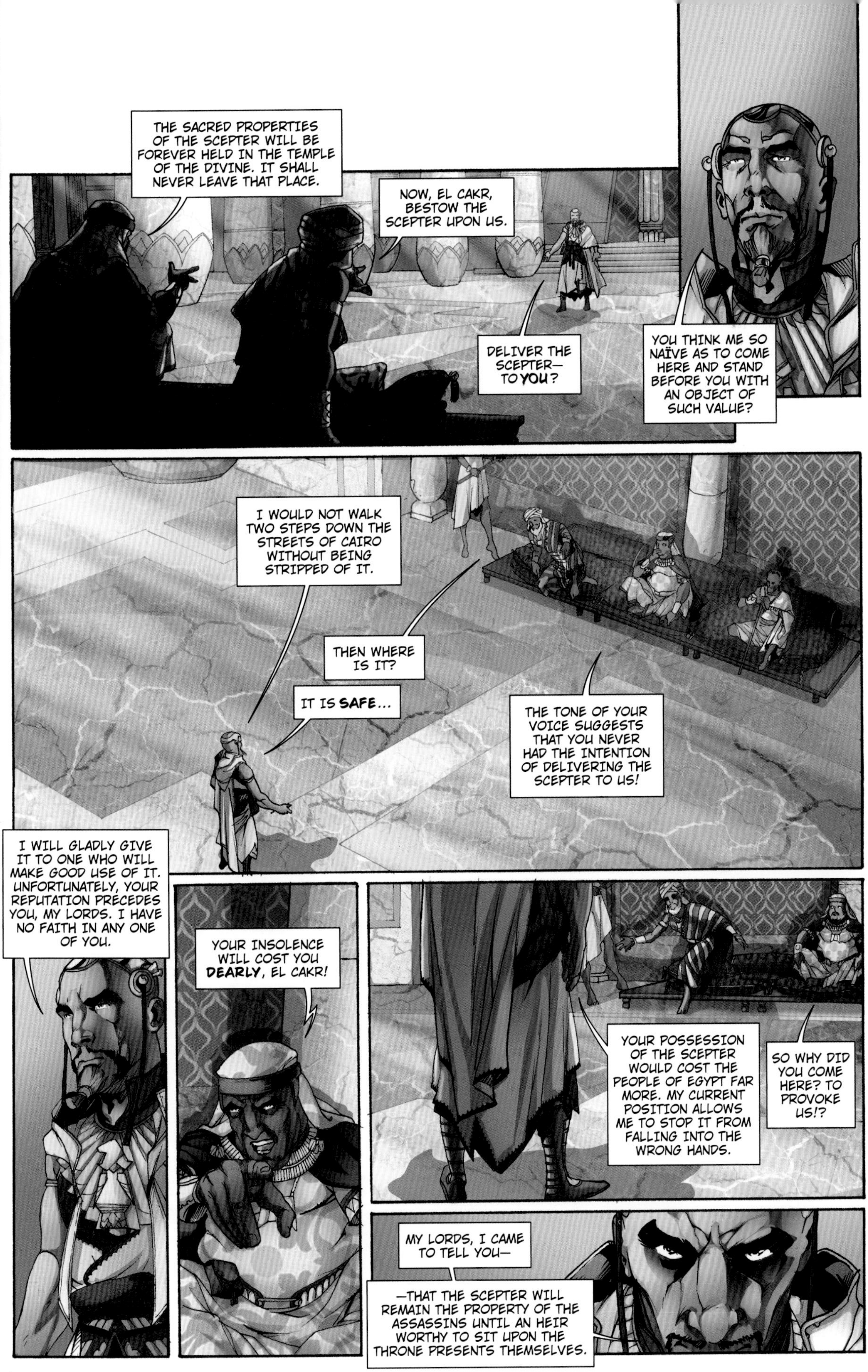
THE SACRED PROPERTIES OF THE SCEPTER WILL BE FOREVER HELD IN THE TEMPLE OF THE DIVINE. IT SHALL NEVER LEAVE THAT PLACE.
NOW, EL CAKR, BESTOW THE SCEPTER UPON US.
DELIVER THE SCEPTER— TO YOU?
YOU THINK ME SO NAÏVE AS TO COME HERE AND STAND BEFORE YOU WITH AN OBJECT OF SUCH VALUE?
I WOULD NOT WALK TWO STEPS DOWN THE STREETS OF CAIRO WITHOUT BEING STRIPPED OF IT.
THEN WHERE IS IT?
IT IS SAFE...
THE TONE OF YOUR VOICE SUGGESTS THAT YOU NEVER HAD THE INTENTION OF DELIVERING THE SCEPTER TO US!
I WILL GLADLY GIVE IT TO ONE WHO WILL MAKE GOOD USE OF IT. UNFORTUNATELY, YOUR REPUTATION PRECEDES YOU, MY LORDS. I HAVE NO FAITH IN ANY ONE OF YOU.
YOUR INSOLENCE WILL COST YOU DEARLY, EL CAKR!
YOUR POSSESSION OF THE SCEPTER WOULD COST THE PEOPLE OF EGYPT FAR MORE. MY CURRENT POSITION ALLOWS ME TO STOP IT FROM FALLING INTO THE WRONG HANDS.
SO WHY DID YOU COME HERE? TO PROVOKE US!?
MY LORDS, I CAME TO TELL YOU—
—THAT THE SCEPTER WILL REMAIN THE PROPERTY OF THE ASSASSINS UNTIL AN HEIR WORTHY TO SIT UPON THE THRONE PRESENTS THEMSELVES.

41

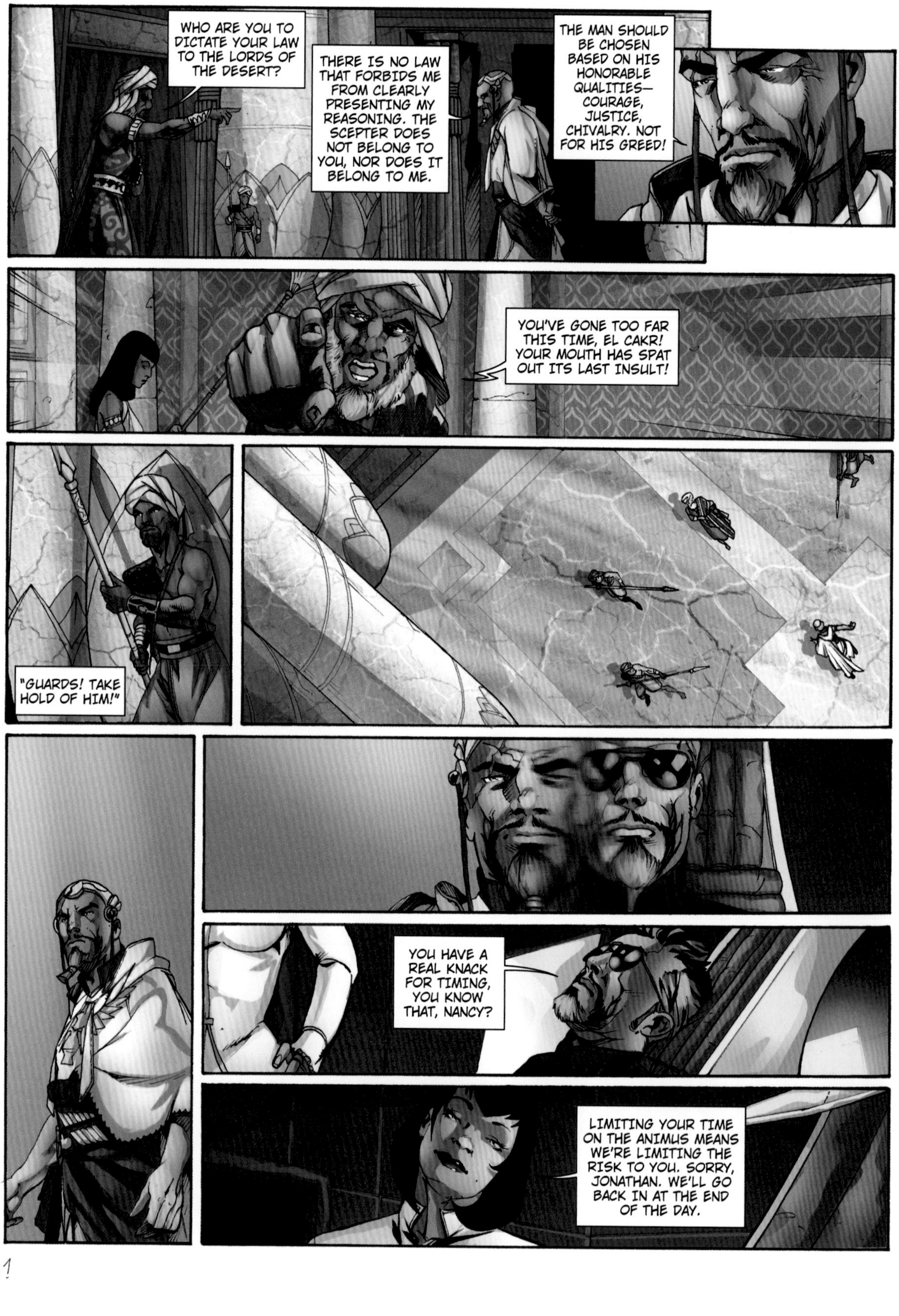
WHO ARE YOU TO DICTATE YOUR LAW TO THE LORDS OF THE DESERT?
THERE IS NO LAW THAT FORBIDS ME FROM CLEARLY PRESENTING MY REASONING. THE SCEPTER DOES NOT BELONG TO YOU, NOR DOES IT BELONG TO ME.
THE MAN SHOULD BE CHOSEN BASED ON HIS HONORABLE QUALITIES—COURAGE, JUSTICE, CHIVALRY. NOT FOR HIS GREED!
YOU'VE GONE TOO FAR THIS TIME, EL CAKR! YOUR MOUTH HAS SPAT OUT ITS LAST INSULT!
"GUARDS! TAKE HOLD OF HIM!"
YOU HAVE A REAL KNACK FOR TIMING, YOU KNOW THAT, NANCY?
LIMITING YOUR TIME ON THE ANIMUS MEANS WE'RE LIMITING THE RISK TO YOU. SORRY, JONATHAN. WE'LL GO BACK IN AT THE END OF THE DAY.

41

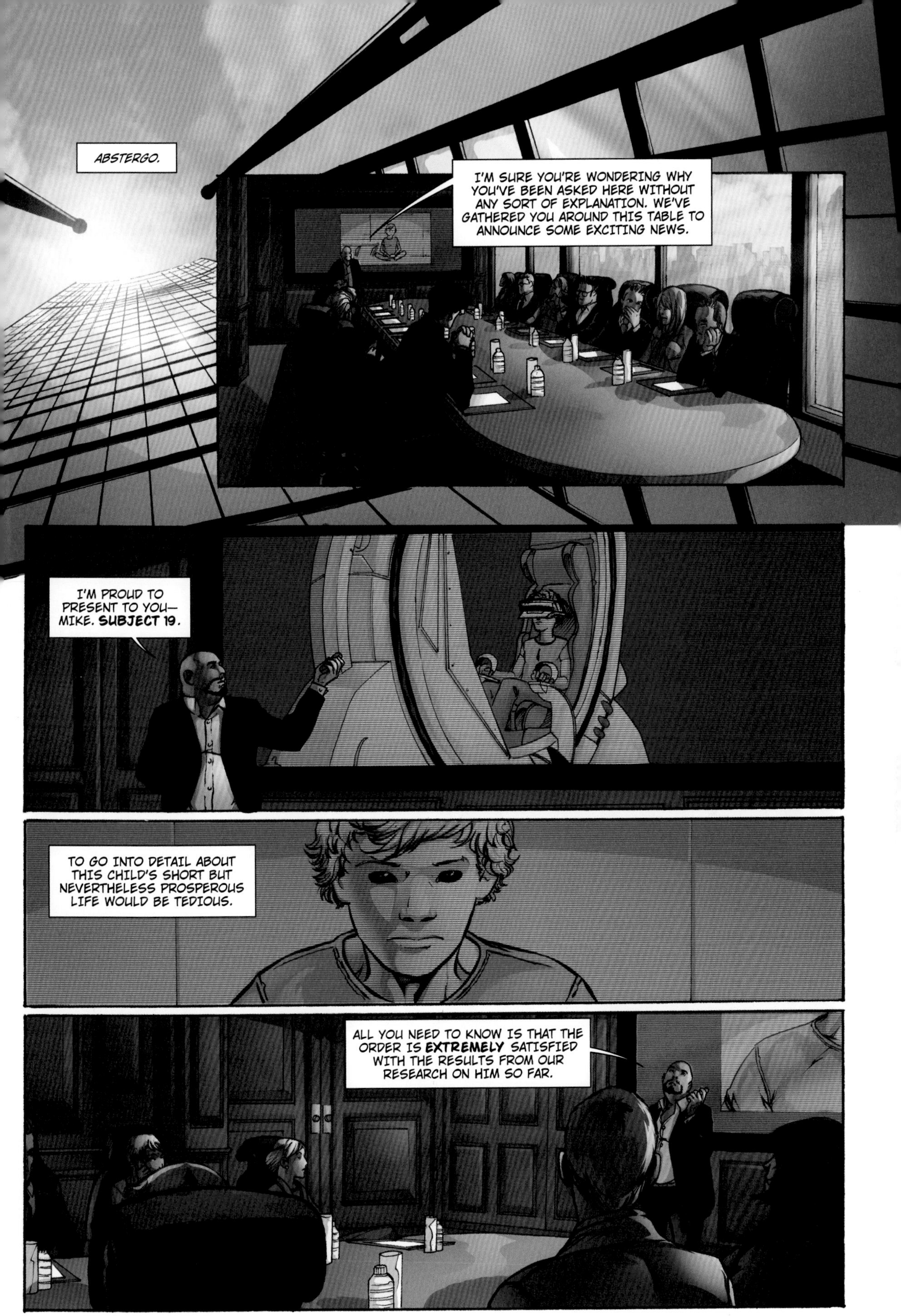
ABSTERGO.
I'M SURE YOU'RE WONDERING WHY YOU'VE BEEN ASKED HERE WITHOUT ANY SORT OF EXPLANATION. WE'VE GATHERED YOU AROUND THIS TABLE TO ANNOUNCE SOME EXCITING NEWS.
I'M PROUD TO PRESENT TO YOU— MIKE. SUBJECT 19.
TO GO INTO DETAIL ABOUT THIS CHILD'S SHORT BUT NEVERTHELESS PROSPEROUS LIFE WOULD BE TEDIOUS.
ALL YOU NEED TO KNOW IS THAT THE ORDER IS EXTREMELY SATISFIED WITH THE RESULTS FROM OUR RESEARCH ON HIM SO FAR.

AFTER MANY YEARS OF STUDY, HARD WORK, AND TRIAL AND ERROR, TODAY WE CAN ANNOUNCE THAT OUR RESEARCHERS HAVE SUCCESSFULLY COMPLETED THE FIRST VIABLE DNA SUPPORT TRANSFER ON A HUMAN BEING...

THIS IMAGE IS CONFIRMATION OF OUR SUCCESS!

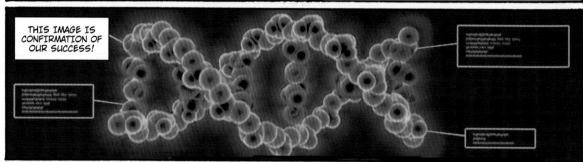

I'LL HAND YOU OVER TO PROFESSOR WILLIAM McCOY, WHO HAS LED THE WORK AND KNOWS MORE ABOUT THE SUBJECT THAN ANYONE. WILL?

TO TELL YOU ABOUT ALL THE PHASES OF THE EXPERIMENT WOULD BE TOO COMPLEX, SO I'LL GIVE YOU THE ESSENTIALS.

THE MOST IMPORTANT THING TO UNDERSTAND IS THAT, TECHNICALLY, MIKE'S MODIFIED DNA IS ABLE TO ASSIMILATE FOREIGN CODES.

OUR LAST TRIAL INVOLVED GRAFTING THE GENETIC HERITAGE OF ONE OF OUR ADVERSARIES ONTO HIS DNA.

WHAT THIS MEANS, IS THAT FROM THIS MOMENT, WE ARE IN A POSITION TO EXPLORE HIS GENETIC MEMORY VIA ALL OF THAT SUBJECT'S ANCESTORS.

IN OTHER WORDS, LADIES AND GENTLEMEN—THE ASSASSIN IS WORKING FOR US!

4

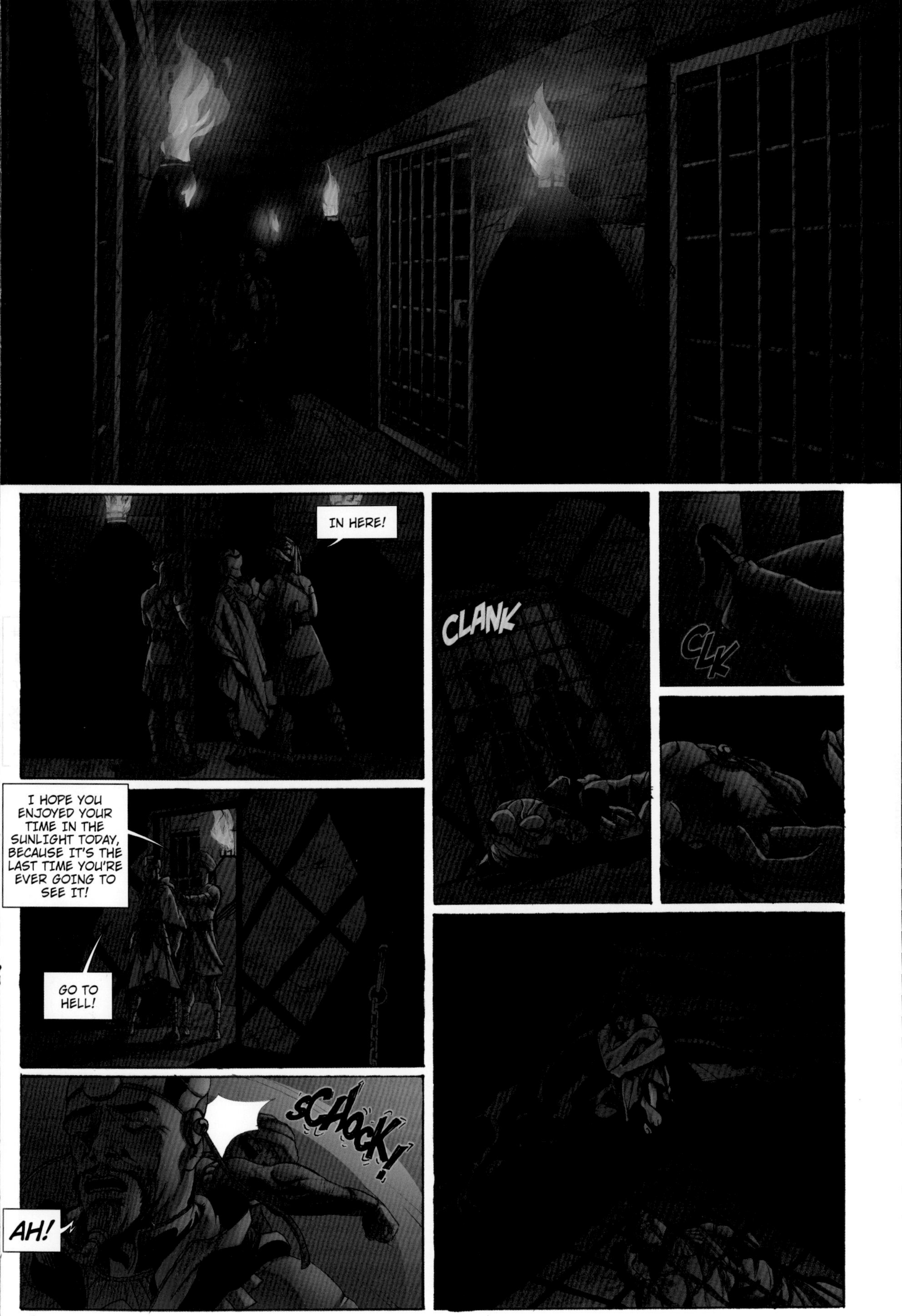
IN HERE!
CLANK
CLK
I HOPE YOU ENJOYED YOUR TIME IN THE SUNLIGHT TODAY, BECAUSE IT'S THE LAST TIME YOU'RE EVER GOING TO SEE IT!
GO TO HELL!
SCHOCK!
AH!

45

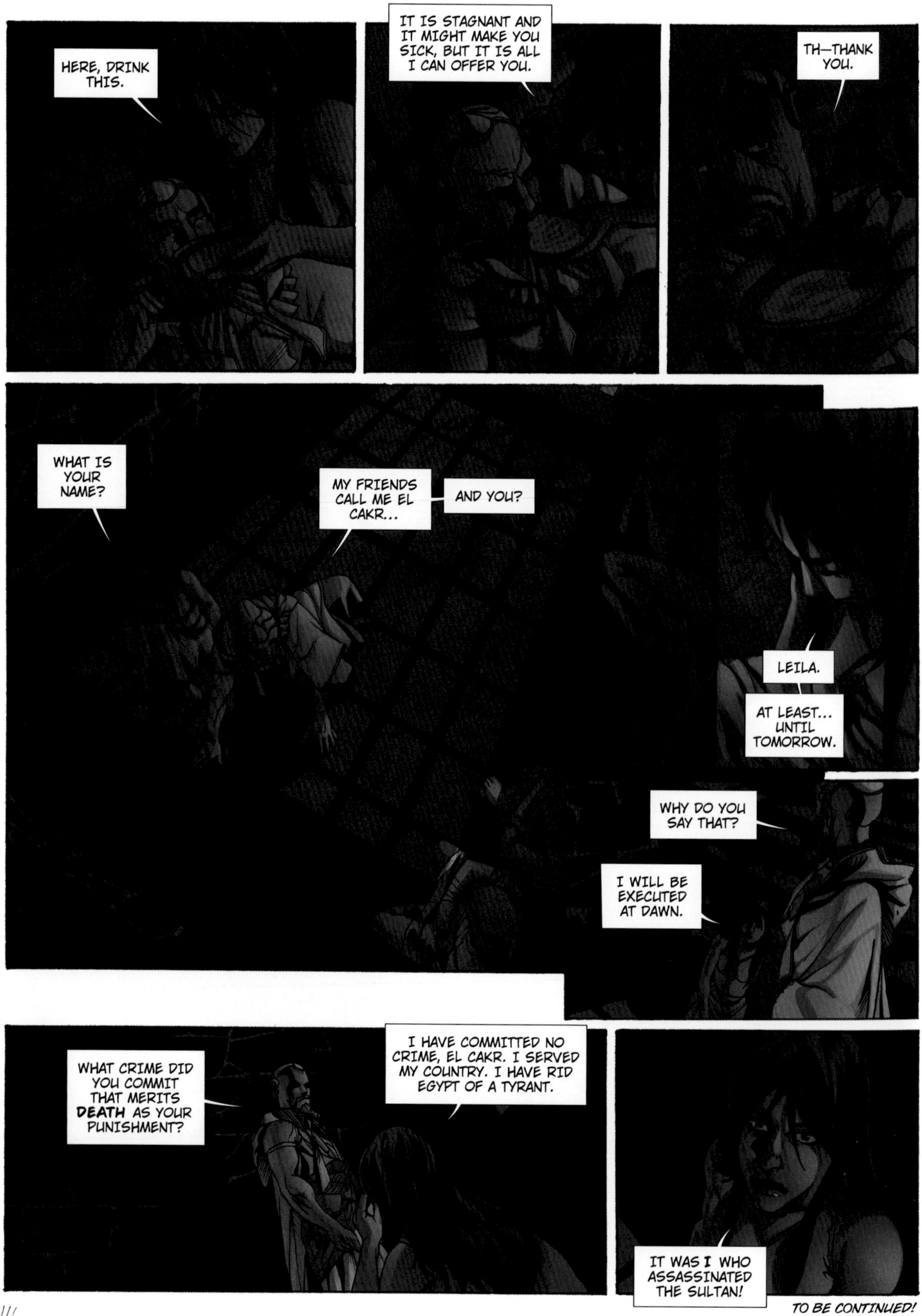

HERE, DRINK THIS.
IT IS STAGNANT AND IT MIGHT MAKE YOU SICK, BUT IT IS ALL I CAN OFFER YOU.
TH—THANK YOU.
WHAT IS YOUR NAME?
MY FRIENDS CALL ME EL CAKR...
AND YOU?
LEILA.
AT LEAST... UNTIL TOMORROW.
WHY DO YOU SAY THAT?
I WILL BE EXECUTED AT DAWN.
WHAT CRIME DID YOU COMMIT THAT MERITS **DEATH** AS YOUR PUNISHMENT?
I HAVE COMMITTED NO CRIME, EL CAKR. I SERVED MY COUNTRY. I HAVE RID EGYPT OF A TYRANT.
IT WAS **I** WHO ASSASSINATED THE SULTAN!

TO BE CONTINUED!